Hunting Hard ... In Alaska!

Book Two

The Soul of the Hunt

Marc Taylor

www.HuntingHardInAlaska.com

i

Other Books by
Marc Taylor:

Hunting Hard...In Alaska!

Book One

"Prepare Yourself to Hunt
'The Last Frontier'"

Hunting Hard...In Alaska!
The Soul of the Hunt

By Marc Taylor

Published by
Hunting Hard – Alaska Adventures
8931 Jupiter Drive
Anchorage, AK 99507-3713
www.HuntingHardInAlaska.com

Copyright© 2006 by Marcus A. Taylor
Published January, 2006

ISBN   0-9726668-1-8
ISBN-13 978-0-9726668-1-7
Library of Congress Control Number: 2005910797

Edited-in-part by Larry Kaniut and Marylin King
Illustrations by Larry Golden of Palmer, Alaska
See final pages for more information on artwork by Larry Golden
Printed in Hong Kong
Cover Design by Foster & Foster, Inc.
Fairfield, Iowa

Dedication

This book is dedicated to those who have assisted in the lighting of this seemingly unquenchable fire.

To my beautiful and loving wife, who has supported my many extended trips and hair-brained schemes. With true display of devotion, SanJuanita has stood by my every endeavor and through my sacrificing of precious time that may have been more suitably spent in the comforts of the wonderful home that she keeps.

To the unconditional love of my two children, Michael and Charla, who from afar have watched as their father disintegrated from a working professional to a driven follower of distant dreams and inspiration. May they someday be fortunate enough to recognize the merits of conventional and unconventional life courses, and choose prosperous and bountiful paths.

To the many friends, mentors, and extended family members who have aided, guided, and pushed me to continue, despite my many very blatant stumbles and direction changes. Your comfort and sincere, objective feedback have paved a wide course for me to travel.

And finally – to Alaska.

I am told very often how fortunate I am to be living my dreams. I invite you to live yours also by allowing Alaska into your soul. One glimpse of its splendor and the hook is set. You'll find yourself fighting for air as you are pulled to its beauty time and time again. To where the tundra rolls endlessly toward distant peaks which hold entrancing powers over the beholder.

Join me in this climb toward heights achieved only by the residents and visitors of "The Great Land", "The Last Frontier"!

You're fighting its power, but you are losing the battle. How do I know, you ask? Because you are holding this book, my friend. Enjoy.

An Invitation

This book supposes that you have read Book One, "Prepare Yourself To Hunt 'The Last Frontier.'" Book Two is the second in a five-part series of books which will inspire those who have never made the journey to take the first step toward making that trip to Alaska. For those of you who have already taken the first step, in the least you now possess memories that will carry beyond your graves.

Book Two is in part a collection of short stories based upon places that I have visited. I felt it was important to portray the hunt through the soul of the hunted as well as through the eyes of the hunter, for the telling of only one side of any story is akin to painting with only one color.

Book Two is also a continuation of our preparations for the hunt. Hunting methods and tactics may remain the same, however, gear utilized and the mind that we enter into the hunt with are constantly being molded and reshaped as we grow in experience and maturity.

I invite you to embrace every moment spent in the company of your quarry. Study their habits and meanderings, dispositions and subtle movements, in order to become more evolved in your adoration for the hunt and the hunted.

In the absence of respect and reverence, ours is but a murderous undertaking. Only on the spiritual level will we be successful in justifying our deeds. And justification is being demanded with ever-increasing fervor. Where once we thrived only because of the success of the hunt, now we fight for the privilege to partake in the hunt. Let's partake while we still can...

Marc with a recent bull moose

Hunting Hard...In Alaska!

Book Two

Foreword
A Soul for the Hunt
By Larry Bartlett

Preface
"Why Do I Hunt?"   1

I. The Ancient Game of Hunter and Hunted   11

The Thousands That Got Away   13
Sealing the Deal   29
Breathless, Under the Weight of a Hunter's Moment   41
The View from an Aspen Grove   45
A Morning in a Mountain Valley Cathedral   63
The Billy Goats' Bluff   73
Broken Instinct   97

II. More on Hunting Gear and Tactics   113

Building a Complete Gear List   115
Sleeping Warm in the Cold   121
Innovative Gear for Hunters   129
When Things Go Terribly Wrong   141
Moose Hunting Tactics – 301   147

III. The Last Breath   157
The Answer to the Question – "Why Do I Hunt?"   159
Photo Gallery   161
A Sense of Belonging   177

IV. Appendix   188

A Soul for the Hunt
By Larry Bartlett

Any given hunt could deliver record breaking results or miserable failure, yet still we're compelled to field duty when opportunity knocks; but why?

For me, hunting is more than killing animals for sport or food. It provides a setting to escape everyday life and offers time for mental and emotional repair, spiritual enlightenment, and humble experiences in Nature. Hunting also broadens awareness to the rhythms of life, which tend to encourage the exploration of one's true self.

Although hunter mentality is a complex subject, hunting desire is more or less a core attraction to a landscape that simply gives more than it gains; and the rewards of engaging Nature provoke our spiritual orientation to life. To put it simpler, the desire to kill is a queer addiction to those who don't hunt, yet an addiction with no cure for those who do.

Reader beware, from here the spiritual wading pool gets deeper and more involved with perceptive reasoning, so roll up your britches and step into the flooding depths of reality that fill our *soul for the hunt.*

Are we to assume that social idealism, religious beliefs, or even genetics help hunters form the shape of their hunting soul? Truthfully, I'm not sold on those choices, so I won't speculate for others. The fact remains, we hunters occasionally interact with

Nature on a non-scientific level, which is rather difficult to explain to someone who has never experienced such euphoria. It provokes an emotion, a positive energy, which cannot be explained with simple logic. Even more cosmic is the possibility of souls (mammal to mammal) interacting through a flow of energy dialed perfectly to connect awareness with acceptance to form enlightenment. To say the least, great comfort exists in spiritual belief.

I recall one hunting moment that involved my spiritual collision with a dying animal and forged a link to my soul for hunting.

August 12, 2000: the assault of proverbial hell was staged at my feet, and the chance for appeal dissolved as the ram's blood seeped down the lichen-covered shale.

My post on the rocky outcrop overlooked a small band of Dall sheep, and my target grazed unaware of his wrong turn. The ram's head filled my scope as I calmly whispered the firing sequence, timing my breathing rate on the count of growth rings: "...seven, eight, nine—exhale...SQUEEZE!"

The bullet struck the animal at the horn base behind its left eye, and the stunning impact jolted the ram's head forward, rebounding like a tightly coiled spring set free. A pink mist dusted the far side rocks, but my focus shifted as the sheep hurled into a backward-dive downslide, folding onto itself, lifeless. That quick my hunt was over, but spiritual awakening closed in fast.

I balanced a camera on a small boulder for a close-up with my trophy, hoping for a nice image to comfort my reflections in old age. I was glowingly proud of the accomplishment, yet unsettled by its bloody demise. The events that followed forever changed my perspectives on shot placement and on life as they relate to death.

In one hand was Ol' *Faithful* (a treasured model 700 Remington .30'06), and in the other rested a peacefully silent nine-year-old ram with an open head wound and glazed eyes. My chest must have bowed like a cunning sniper after his first kill. However, the building chaos was not that of a combat mission, but rather a real-time fight or flight scenario about to be jammed into fast-foreword play. The surprise, which stirred silently in my grasp, would ground my ego and test my defenses.

The shaggy white skin covering the ram's muscles began to quiver like a birddog on point. I recall hesitating long enough to dismiss the muscle movements as residual impulses from a damaged central nervous system (common with head and spine injuries). But in reality intuition had failed me, because all signs pointed to a frightened soul trapped between two worlds—life and death—as the sheep resurrected violently within my unsuspecting clutch.

Later inspection would reveal a pass-through bullet hole about ¼-inch up the horn base, which inflicted just enough crushing shock to result in temporary death-like symptoms. That is, it remained unconscious just long enough for me to be cradling its head and horns, posing for a photo, before awakening to kick my ass.

Imagine my surprise!

An assault took form, but luckily I managed to work my legs into a scissor-lock around the ram's chest cavity before it could regain its footing. And with a forearm stretched through its horn curvature, I forced the head and neck backward to try controlling the thrashing convulsions. My instincts took command with logic on its heels, convincing me that suffocation would deliver the quickest death.

I still believe I made the right decision, yet I was humbled by the animal's dying strength.

So there we were, locked together as a thrashing duo of spiritual chaos and bloody massacre. I struggled painfully to keep the ram's horns back against its spine with my strongest arm, while my left hand gripped the muzzle with crushing force to seal the airway. Meanwhile, the sheep heaved desperately for air, and its futile attempts resulted in combative leg assaults. I felt contact with every other kick as the sharp edges of its front hooves chiseled into my shin. Scree shards punctured my backside with every twist. The battle drained me quickly, and I prayed desperately for Divine intervention with every conscious thought.

The awkward struggle joined us close in arms, leading to eye contact. A primal force within me was repulsed by the urge to look away, as if I would be turning my back on a moral duty. So I trusted this emotion and searched deeply into the golden-hazel starburst that pulsed black with a dancing pupil. Shame and sorrow, perhaps even fear, consumed my thoughts as I studied the facing eye for a signal to the end.

Mammals have an extraordinary ability to communicate through eye contact, and this was the connection my emotions seemed to prefer.

My strength was fading and the animal's physiological demand for air seemed endless. I rejected my body's urge to release the grip on its muzzle; and so continued the fight, until several minutes later when its body accepted defeat and its spirit the final leg to death (brain cells cannot survive without a constant re-supply of fresh oxygen).

Almost as if the ram sensed he was fighting in vain, an overwhelming calmness swept through its gaze. It was a message of pure relief, acceptance, and strangely enough, forgiveness. I used this perception later for spiritual closure, albeit suspicious of accurate translation. I then wondered if this communication was nothing more than my own guilt transferring wrong doing to resolution for emotional closure. While this is one possible explanation of the supernatural connection, faith is more powerful than science in this argument.

From there I felt the slow decline of the ram's energy. Its carcass fell limp in my cramping arms. I wept, trying to absorb the facts of the ordeal and praying for forgiveness and reason. I also struggled to make sense by replaying the events on a mental loop.

That loop continued to dominate my concentration for days thereafter, until I admitted error with my shot placement and reprimanded myself through shameful self-doubt—retribution for insurance against repeat offenses.

Damaged emotions were all that remained of my strength at that point, so I guess I had reached the rock bottom of my spiritual cache. Some people believe that God is responsible for all such forms of suffering, which serves to encourage our spiritual development. Regardless of the fact, I recovered from that episode to be more compassionate, respectful, and wise to life on a natural level, which continues to enhance my spiritual enlightenment. Perhaps I had simply tapped into a realm of the human conscience that calls us to action to explore our spiritual boundaries. This exploration most certainly cuts the heart to reveal truth and twists the gut to hide fear, motivating us to evolve. Furthermore, it was clear that one man's reality is another man's insanity, just the same as one man's acceptance is someone else's judgment.

Science has taught us that everything in Nature is balanced by equal opposites, which suggests that everything with a top has a bottom and that which is living must also die. A few proverbial examples are the *yin* and *yang*; the *flip* and *flop;* and the absolute *is* and *was.*

By using scientific logic laced with spiritual faith, I now believe that balance of all things in Nature must have equal opposites. Although I struggle to explain, much less prove the connection made that day, I cannot deny its balance of fact. The emotional impact humbled me to weakness and nurtured me back to strength by sharpening my senses of Nature's energetic balance.

Perhaps vulnerability itself was God's true gift to me that day. I suppose if any good resulted, life was not wasted. Most certainly, the meat from that ram was treated with the highest regard and offered succulence beyond description.

Granted, the written experience is difficult to embrace without forming judgment, but the sobering effect of this torment impressed personal insignificance long enough to be granted spiritual enlightenment. My soul became stronger.

Was I righteous? Should I celebrate the experience or beg forgiveness for my actions?

Answers to these questions (and others like it) are found most often while hunting, which possibly fuel our craving for the next adventure but definitely enrich our hunting spirit through conscience and morality. These are the fundamentals known to embody our *soul* for hunting.

Many hunters believe that a *soul* is the interaction of logic with our moral compass, which guides ethical hunting practices and is policed by spiritual self-check. Basic fear of Divine retribution is another explanation. Righteous duty is another possibility. As hunters, we use the soul to embrace a primal urge to kill, which implies a soul reveals the spiritual bounty in our experiences, commands our respect for a Divine authority, and commits us to honor the animals' spirit through good will (uncompromising field technique); all this in preparation to enjoy its flesh as a gift from Nature. Regardless of outside perceptions, all hunters eventually find themselves in quandaries where moral guidance is the only hope for salvation, and only then may our moral character and hunting soul be fulfilled.

Our conscience, however linked to the soul, is a blend of personality traits and emotional intuition, which program individual behaviors through life. A conscience is developed from birth, then shaped by moral guidance, and continues to lead our actions of good will. Therefore, when matters of right and wrong are challenged within us, this *feeling* is thought to be driven by our conscience. Without such moral counter measures, the more unlikely it would be to possess a soul for the hunt.

I believe the fundamental traits of one's *soul for hunting* are clearly defined as being competitive; achieving confidence; displaying courage; refining good will; refusing failure; cultivating intellect; and serving Nature with honor. Each trait possibly lends a certain degree of wanderlust to that hunter, as the excitement of new possibilities build to anticipation for the next hunt. Therefore, a hunter's soul is likely compelled by Nature, challenged by mystery, and only temporarily satiated by hunting adventure.

The soul for hunting is a compelling force that is difficult to explain but impossible to deny. However, it must be individually recognized before it can benefit the individual. Comprehension of such a complex subject is a matter of individual practices and repetitive exercise, so it then becomes a right of passage to be explored by others like you. Once harnessed, the spiritual reflection of hunting invokes a certain wisdom that stirs desire, provides solace, and provokes emotional closure with our field experiences.

That is the best way I can explain how we hunters deal with taking the lives of our prey. Non-hunters likely call this justification, but I prefer to think of it as exercising our soul for hunting.

If this subject is appealing, then you'll likely receive tremendous pleasure from the pages that follow. Like me, Marc Taylor lives by the *soul for the hunt*; but more importantly, he has great passion and respect for life, which guide his talent to put pen to paper and food on the table. Taylor has an uncanny way to capture the thoughts we privately explore but fail miserably to explain.

After reading *Book One* of the *Hunting Hard* series, I was compelled to learn more about Marc's spiritual hunting impressions. I view this book's theme as the beginning to a long reader relationship Marc Taylor will have to endure. This book satisfies my craving for shared hunting experiences, and it lends the hindsight wisdom of a willing hunter who skillfully explores the shadows of his own soul with impressive candor. It's about time another enlightened hunter joined the Alaska writing scene. Now, we are not alone with bawling tears when the ego-crushing moments in Nature compel us to seek truth. His vicarious wisdom encourages us to seek and survive the struggles of hunting hard in Alaska. His hunting and writing styles come naturally from the heart, but his stroke is all soul. If your escape from the preoccupations in life begins with hunting, continue to study your own reflections on Nature for enlightenment. After reading this book, search the wilds for your own soul for the hunt. You might also share your passionate experiences with those you love, knowing that the evolution of hunting requires food for thought. Good hunting!

—Larry Bartlett

Fairbanks, Alaska

Author of *A Complete Guide to Float Hunting Alaska* and *Caribou Hunting: A Guide to Alaska's Herds*. Larry is currently working on video productions and a new book, which promise more soulful reflections and how-to hunting knowledge.

Among hunters, Larry Bartlett is a warrior! Thanks for the help – *Marc*

The Question – "Why Do I Hunt?"

You cringe as the question leaves his or her lips – not because you don't have the answer but because you feel that in moments you will be defending yourself, your passions and your past. The room becomes a blur and everyone seems to await your response now in slow motion.

The thoughts race but collide on the way to your tongue. After much reading on the past, present and future of hunting; maybe after some form of rehearsal as to what your answer might be, when, and not if, this happens again – you draw a blank. Certainly not out of fear of stumbling, fear of ridicule, or fear of not providing the answer that this person may be expecting of you, but because you know that the answer is very complex and not something that can be defended or explained in a sentence or even a mere paragraph.

So the really meaningful words escape you at that most critical of times. Just like when your wife or girlfriend asks, "Why do you love me?" You've thought about that particular question one thousand and one times, but you just cannot convey it with the slick reasoning of a politician explaining away the new taxes that he is proposing.

In a quiet moment not too long after the dreaded question, not long after the inappropriate answer that you may have delivered, you reflect on questions of your own.

"Why do we hunt?" you ask yourself. Then, if your insight is deep enough, your questions begin to flow.

What must go through the mind of that hunter as he prepares to end the life of another of the earth's creatures? Why does he choose that particular creature to hunt?

Surely the hunter recognizes the natural physical beauty of the animal about to be taken. Could it be that the value of the meat and the value of the memories the hunt will create are greater to the hunter than the value of the animal's right to exist to fulfill its own destiny? And what of the destiny of that game animal... are we selfish enough to think that is it to fulfill the basic need of the hunter for food and warmth?

I can assure you that I have never had game animals line up at the end of my rifle barrel to fulfill their destiny. Most are taken unaware of my presence and in the case that my presence is revealed, I have yet to experience an animal surrender his life for my desires. If the game animal could answer, I wager that its purpose would be... to thrive and then to die naturally within its environment.

Simply put, our actions show that we have placed the value of human life above the value of the lives of the remaining inhabitants of the earth. As human beings, we are taught that to kill another of *our own* species for pleasure, sport, or without a cause deemed just in our collective thinking is against *human nature.* Such action would not further the guarantee of *human* survival. *Our* fulfillment; our procreation and *our* continuance.

The fact that evolution has provided game animals with the defenses necessary to endure the elements without shelter should tip us to the fact that the animals we hunt are also here to survive; for *their* fulfillment; *their* procreation and continuance.

So, why do we extend protection to some inhabitants of the planet but not to others?

Do the physical similarities of humans alone afford us any protection from each other as hunters?

Humans walk upright. This alone sets us apart from other creatures on the planet. But what do you suppose would happen if a hunter or hiker came across an animal similar in characteristics – but misplaced; something like the fabled 'Sasquach', or 'Yeti'?

The human would probably shoot it!

The shooter would then claim that he could not identify with it, and shot it because he felt "threatened". "Hey, the 'Sasquach' was circling me in a puzzled way and uttering guttural sounds! I had to shoot it before it attacked me!" That would be the claim.

So much for physical characteristics affording protection.

What of the ability to reason or make decisions? Is that a consideration when deciding which species' to hunt? Do we think that we are hunting "dumb" animals that are far inferior to us as humans?

Animals can be taught to make decisions on a basic level, and some animals reason without being taught. We, as humans, of course, call that reasoning *instinct* – a knowledge that must have been passed down genetically through birth. Humans have convinced themselves that if animals communicate knowledge in any other way than just handing it down genetically, they would possess intelligence, thus making them "smart"; capable of thought. We choose not to believe that the inferior creatures of this planet are capable of thought, so we convince ourselves that animals act on instinct alone.

A few of us are not convinced.

Anyone with modest time spent afield will attest that some animals possess sensory abilities that humans can only dream of. If a human were to possess even one tenth of the strength, hearing, smell, or sight capability of the keenest of the animal world, that person would be known to possess "super-human" abilities.

We are hunting creatures with superior abilities in most cases, and it's a good thing that the more dangerous of them doesn't actively hunt us. We must appreciate them for their abilities – as we hunt them for their meat and adorning headgear.

How dreadfully uneventful it would be to hunt animals possessing mere human senses!

All animals have a place within the contained, life-sustaining planet that we as humans have claimed as ours to dominate, but I guess it's up to us to decide whose place is where...

So, why do we spare some from the bullet and broad head, but not others?

We are searching here, but there is a simple answer quite easily reached. Just examine the protection afforded the animals that we have domesticated to serve and to comfort us.

Your family pet *communicates* the desire to please and serve you by anticipating and acting upon your commands, and it demonstrates the desire to have you provide for its needs. In return, you spare it from harm. You are *communicating* with your pet, conditioning it to respond to your desires. It is also conditioning you to respond to its desires. Just try ignoring that whimper you get when the dog *needs* to be let out!

Therefore, it must be the ability and willingness to *communicate* with us that spares a species from the gun or bow. We have spared the animals that respond to our communication efforts. Those animals we surround ourselves with and nurture as companions.

In the remainder of creatures we find beauty, value, nourishment, or uniqueness that makes them targets of our pursuit. Hey, what hunter wouldn't want the head and shoulders of a beautiful Dall sheep ram hanging in his living room? What a testament that must be to his ability to dominate the "lesser" creatures within the reach of his budget and bullet!

Again: *Why do I hunt?*

Eliminate sustenance alone from the root of the answer to the question, because it is known and accepted in some human societies that the meat of the dog, domestic or wild, is among the tastiest of meats. If you are truly hunting for meat alone, then there it is – meat for a week – curled and resting at your feet, or purring in your lap.

Most of us work for a living, and can reasonably afford to visit the grocery store within a short distance from our homes, so hunting for meat, alone, is not the answer – especially after we pay the fees and expenses involved in the hunting, transporting, processing and storage of the meat that we bring to the table in the name of subsistence.

There is something even greater than our desire to provide protein to our bodies. Sure, providing meat for the pot is real, and there is little more satisfying than enjoying the fruits of our labors. We can see the flesh of our conquest; taste it, and it sustains us.

But there is something else, isn't there?

We are now going to reach deep within ourselves. We will search far beyond our claims that we eat what we hunt, to reveal the other motive for our pursuits of the fair creatures of this lovely planet.

Remember when you were a child holding your first BB gun? What was the feeling - *the power* – it gave you? You weren't satisfied just shooting the tin cans that your father set up for you. Remember how you used that power against a little bird in your yard? I do.

Were you experiencing the power to decide life and death?

I also remember sobbing in shame as I laid that first conquest to rest under three inches or so of soil in my grandfather's barn. I didn't understand what caused me to take the life of that bird, and I felt some disgrace for having done it; but as the sorrow wore off with the passing of a short amount of time I wanted to do it again. And again. I had learned – self taught – that I had power over the other creatures within my environment.

Is that a good thing?

With those simple lessons I was learning skills that would

later allow me to accomplish greater things, and before long, I was knocking squirrels from the tree tops and tumbling rabbits in the bushes. Progression and encouragement led to the taking of my first deer, and I remember the celebration that followed.

It was a kind of commencement; a kind of graduation. Hunting had taken hold of me.

Even as the meat of my first deer lingered in the deep-freezer, I couldn't wait for the opportunity to take another one. And maybe if I were lucky enough to get a shot at a truly big buck, that would elevate me to the revered status of an *accomplished* hunter.

Recall the envy you felt when that other youngster your age downed the nine-point buck, and you were trying to hang on to the pride you felt at having taken a spike-fork? Then someone came up and slapped you on the back and said, "You can't eat antlers, son."

You wanted to believe it, but there was that beaming grin on the other kid's face. Next time around, you wanted possession of that big grin.

You had begun to experience "hunting pressure" – the pressure not only to be successful at the hunt, but to be *accomplished*; and accomplishment was now a part of the hunting experience. No, it became a *goal* of the hunting experience.

At about this time the young hunter passes from a learning hunter, having broken away from "Uncle So-and-So" or whomever the mentoring force was that helped to light the fire.

He changes into a killing machine, bent on killing more deer than any of his friends, and not only more of them, but bigger ones. This particular phase hopefully will be relatively short-lived, and will usually cause rules to be bent or broken in the process. Most of us overcome that mentality but some do not.

At this point there must be an intervening force. It may be a mentoring by a more evolved hunter, or a single experience that will speed the evolution of the young hunter into a respectful, reverent being.

My evolution took place in an afternoon. Maybe you had a similar experience:

From a tree stand I shot a young buck as it fed. I left my rifle at the base of the tree for some reason and tracked the deer through thick brush to a small clearing where it lay as if resting. It *lay*, with legs tucked under its body as I approached. I knelt in front of it at a distance of maybe three feet. The deer looked right through me. It was breathing normally, blinking and chewing its cud as if nothing had happened. The right side of the deer, which was the side that I shot, was not visible and there was no blood on the trail that I had followed to the spot. I began to question whether I had hit it at all, and whether I was actually kneeling there in front of a mature whitetail that was looking right through me. This all seemed like a dream. I was seemingly invisible to this deer lying three feet in front of me.

I was staring into the eyes of the deer, and I could see my reflection on its glossy orbs; that was the only affirmation I had that this wasn't a dream.

As I knelt before it, the buck then gurgled and spit up blood all over the ground. I fell backward in surprise and horror as the deer started to bay – loudly, as if calling for its distant mother.

I began to bawl. I ran to get my rifle in order to put this deer out of its misery as soon as possible. I could hear it crying as I charged back to my tree stand. When I returned, moments later, the young buck lay dead.

Thank God I didn't have to hear it cry for life – or death – anymore.

That afternoon changed my life forever. I had caused the death of animals on many occasions, but had never experienced the death as I had on that day.

After an experience such as that, it's a wonder that a hunter would continue to hunt at all. I overcame the moment that I had with the deer on that sunny afternoon, but I then carried with me a new respect for the life-taking passion that we call hunting.

For some, causing death is undertaken with the same feeling as pulling on a pair of socks. But our evolution was driven by our experiences, and experience tells me that humans at one time did, and some still do, hunt for meat alone. Explain then, the petroglyphs drawn on rocks in caves, depicting the hunter and the hunted engaging in the act. Those were drawn out of love for the experience and reverence for the hunted, we can be assured. We don't see pictures of meat caches, we see the hunt. Were they attempting to capture memories?

I have my hunting memories to thank for my new-found appreciation of the moment of death, and I now deal death with much more thought having been applied to what will be a very final outcome for the hunted.

I have asked many questions of myself in search of the answer to what should be a simple question... Why?

I write this in a state that is far from what any man would consider wealthy, but I am able to afford the groceries at the store down the street; yet I choose to exercise my position in the food chain... Why?

I eat what I hunt, which limits the amount of money that I spend at that grocery store, but I spend thousands of dollars a year flying to remote places to gather meat and memories. Very possibly, this causes me to spend more than necessary to feed my family... Why?

So why do I hunt?

Well, I'll tell you why... First I want you to take a glimpse into my soul. This book will culminate with the reasons that I hunt. Maybe you'll do some soul searching along the way as well, and forever change the way you approach the hunt. One thing is for certain, what you are about to read will surely change the way you will want to read about it.

– Don't "poach" by skipping to the back of the book!
Enjoy.

Part I

The Ancient Game
of
"Hunter and Hunted"

The Thousands That Got Away

No banking or slipping; as a matter of fact, not much jostling at all. This turbine-charged *DeHavilland Otter* is smooth. Four caribou hunters and enough gear for a comfortable stay in a base camp cruise along twelve hundred feet above wet Alaska tundra. The droning of the Otter's powerful engine is barely heard by the daydreaming expeditioners as they cruise along.

Necks are strained as brown bears and caribou are viewed on the passing tundra below. The caribou, dozens in number, meander in seemingly aimless fashion toward a distant destination, and the bears forage the tundra for marmots and the plump, rain-fed blueberries. *It shouldn't be long*, one hunter thinks, as he glances over at his buddy who is beaming with a wide grin from behind a camcorder – he's recording the flight for grandchildren not yet born.

Retractable wheels on the floats give the amphibious plane the ability to take off from a hard-surfaced runway and deliver hunters and gear to an alpine lake pretty much in the middle of nowhere; or anywhere for that matter, as its fuel capacity allows travel over great expanses. You could say it's the Cadillac of bush planes.

...if only Cadillac's could fly.

This was turning out to be a truly memorable flight, having originated in Dillingham, Alaska. Native Alaskans consider Dillingham a large village, but to most non-natives it's a small town at the silty confluence of the Wood and Nushagak Rivers. The village, or town, depending on your bloodline or reference of thinking, is a popular jumping-off point for the famous and the obscure bound for getaways in lavish hunting and fishing lodges, or just the humble drop-camp preferred by frugal, more rudimentary adventurers.

The panel-mounted GPS, utilized as a navigational aid by the pilot, shows thirteen minutes of flight time remaining to the lake where the hunters will spend the next week in pursuit of the ranging caribou of the Mulchatna herd. This excursion has been well planned, and most every possible detail has been thought out. The hunters, being Alaska residents, chose not to hire a professional guide to assist them in the everyday details of the hunt, but to hire an air guide in order to be put in a position where they might have a reasonable chance to contact game. It is the first such adventure for three of the hunters, but very familiar to the fourth, having hunted this herd, and coincidentally this general location on a previous, very successful caribou hunt.

The great Otter begins to descend gently gliding effortlessly over a long, placid lake in the picturesque, low mountains of Southwest Alaska. The seasoned pilot eases back on the throttle while applying flaps, and now the great amphibious plane floats mere feet from the glassy lake, its pontoons longing to settle into the icy-cold, clear water like the legs of a flaring swan reaching out for the pond. A light rain pelts the windshield.

The plane splashes down, sending spray outward and behind. In unison the hunters look around at each other and smiles emerge from previously taut lips. The last moments before landing are unusually long-lasting as the expectation of the splash always precedes the actual event with exaggerated, tense anticipation.

What was aircraft is now watercraft, taxiing feverishly toward a narrow beach made of granite and jade gravel. The coordinated manipulation of the water rudders, throttle and pitch of the prop steer the plane to the intended beaching point. The floats bump the bottom and the pilot turns his head back to his passengers – a chewed, unlit cigar juts from the side of a suntanned grin.

You know, everyone is happy when a float plane comes to a safe landing on a lake in the middle of *Nowhere*, Alaska.

The herd feeds lazily in and out of a broken patch of alder and willow. The migration has begun and the great bull with the torn right ear senses that the mass of bodies will continue the journey soon. For now, he rests on a mound of tussocks and lichen, re-chewing the morning's sustenance. He is surrounded by five lesser caribou bulls, but three are not "lesser" by much.

The large, branching antlers that adorn the great bull rise nearly four feet above his head. Growing from massive bases, his main beams sweep back and up in a great arc, accentuated with wide palms and long daggers of antler jutting upward and back from the thick trunks. His sight is slightly obstructed above and forward of his nose by the two blades that split his vision. He can just glimpse the arms and hands of bone that are above his ears. They hover above him as constant reminders of the heavy weight he has been blessed – or cursed – to travel with.

He is a sight to behold, even for others of his kind, with a mane of pure white hair stretching from the lower part of his jaw to nearly the center of his back. The remainder of his pelt is the color of the unlikely mingling of charcoal and cinnamon.

The great bull has made this journey many times, and has rested near this very spot in at least one of the three occasions that they have traveled through this particular valley.

They wait for the mood of the herd to shift back into the travel mode. The wait won't be long, for the tremendous herd, nearing two thousand in number, never pauses for very long. They travel at a driven pace – driven by the large pack of wolves that occasionally closes to claim the young or weak, and driven by the desire to reach the familiar fall mating grounds.

It is a yearly ritual, and the paths are ingrained into the memory of the youngest of the herd. Soon, they will lead their young, and then theirs will follow, faithfully, just as it has been for many thousands of years.

There comes the sensation of a current of water shifting, an ebb tide pulling toward the sea now, and the herd is up and moving again.

The pace remains slow for the time being as the caribou of the massive herd, half-grazing and half-trotting, move out to the southeast. A wind blows from the direction of travel, beckoning them to its source. The wind is an ally. It keeps the hordes of flies, mosquitoes, and gnats at bay, they're unable to keep up with the pace of the animals and fight the wind currents simultaneously. The flies are ever present at this time of the year; rains providing nourishing moisture to once dormant larvae.

The herd climbs a low pass separating two mountainous ridges. A number of mature cows, their yearlings and calves in tow, lead the way. The cows are the matriarchs of the herd. In possession of the seeds of future herds as well as the knowledge of past ventures, they push through and over the valleys and tundrous plateaus of this west-central range of mountains. *Press on. The clock is ticking. We have much farther to travel before we reach the wind-blown mating ground.*

Bulls are intermingled throughout the herd, each attempting to keep track of a small harem of females. The largest of the bulls are traveling in the back third of the mass of animals. For them, with larger body masses and heavy antlers, the trip is more grueling. A few will fall to predators, and only the strongest, most able will reach the destination year after year. The great bull is among those at the back of the pack. With each passing year that the trip is made, he falls farther and farther from the front-runners.

A wide valley looms in the distance. The valley contains a rather large lake, stretching from the base of the mountains at the northern end of the valley to the open tundra to the south. With no current, the lake is the perfect training pool for teaching the smaller animals to swim. Many wide rivers are in the path of the herd, and the younger animals must master the art of swimming before they negotiate the treacherous currents.

At this pace, we will reach the water before dark.

A light rain falls in the valley of the lake.

The pilot climbs from an open hatch and walks the left float to the beach.   There he rotates the propeller, as instructed coincidentally by the large sticker on the cowling of the plane which reads, "Rotate propeller after shutting down engine."   He then pulls up his hip- waders, wades back to the tail and with a slight tug, dislodges the huge aircraft, turning it so that the rudder-end of the floats are touching the beach just below the surface of the water.   That will allow him a quick getaway.

The hunters rush to unload the gear from the Otter.   The pilot passes the bags, containers, and rifles down to the float, where another hunter awaits to pass them to shore.   On the gravel shore the bags are placed under a tarp to keep the rain from soaking the items that have not been waterproofed.   Hunters should always expect gear to be rained *on* in Alaska.

"The caribou will come from the North and West", shouts the pilot, "and can pass through here at any time".

"How many can we expect to see?" asks one hunter, as he digs into his pack for his rain bottoms.

"Could be a couple hundred, or it could be a couple thousand. The plateau above this lake is a major thoroughfare for the herds traveling north.   I've put lots of camps on this lake, and you should all have shooting opportunities.   I'll be back on Tuesday. Good luck!"

The hunters now scramble to erect tents in a steady rain.

The pilot, with the unlit cigar still jutting from his mouth, climbs back through the small hatch to the left of his seat. Almost immediately the engine comes to life and with one nudge of the throttle the plane pulls away from the beach and is again waterborne. The hunters are pelted with sideways spray, and the tarp flies from the gear as if blown by a gale-force wind.

The turbine-charged engine screams as the Otter races away from the beach. In less than one hundred and fifty yards it is airborne. The hunters stand in the rain, entranced by the power and beauty of the craft that has transported them to this remote destination. There are very few who do not stare in awe when the aircraft that is your sole connection with civilization leaves you... alone, on a beach, in the middle of *Nowhere*, Alaska.

And the pilot, experiencing "just another day at the office", will be home in time for supper with his wife.

Tents are finally up and gear is for the most part dry. It's a bit late in the afternoon, so the boys get to making individual suppers. The usual freeze-dried dinners, with maybe some jerky or a handful of nut-and-granola trail mix on the side. The rain subsides for a while and the hunters remove themselves from the tents to examine the hunting area from the perspective of new arrivals.

The view from outside the tent is breathtaking at the least. Nishlik Lake, reflecting the sky's light like a mirror, stretches before them to the south, with mountains reaching right into the water on the western shore. A wide shelf of tundra is on the east, with a ridge that stretches the length of the lake, but inland from it nearly a mile. Runoff streams feed the greater body of water from springs that seep from mountainsides. Mighty aquifers that supply them run deep and cold beneath the earth's crust. Surely that is where life began – from the purest of the planet's sources.

All rain has ceased, but the clouds still loom overhead. The hunters emerge in turn, having stowed gear within tents and readied sleeping bags and mats for the chilly night ahead. Very little is said as each hunter turns in a complete circle, taking in the full beauty of his surroundings. The silence was deafening, and then a lake trout breaks the surface of the mirror to grab an unfortunate fly. "I can have him in one cast!" boasts one of the hunters. "Somebody get a fire going, would you?"

Not five minutes following the first disturbance, the surface of glass is broken again, this time by the fly on the end of a cast fishing line. The nymph sinks very slowly, being held in suspension by tiny air bubbles trapped within meticulously placed hairs.

A lighted wad of duct tape is placed beneath a loosely placed pile of damp driftwood, and fire is born.

The sight of the foreign, tantalizing imitation is too much for the dark brown adult female trout, which blasts toward it with one mighty whip of her tail. The hunter, turned fisherman, whips the rod toward the dark gray sky at the vibration caused by the fly being jerked from its descent. The fight is short lived, and there is succulent, steaming flesh of fire-roasted trout being pulled from pin bones not an hour later.

The hunt is already successful, and the hunters linger by the light and warmth of the fire until late in the evening.

The leading caribou of the herd reach the near shore of the lake that splits the wide valley. Without hesitation, they descend the shallow bluff surrounding the water's edge, which is guarded by thick alder growth. Wide, cloven hooves create churning white water as the surface of the placid lake is shattered like glass. The water is cold, but its chill is unnoticed by the densely coated caribou, whose hollow hairs lend buoyancy as powerful legs gyrate to propel the animals forward at a pace envious to even an Olympic swimmer.

The tumultuous roar of splashing water is replaced with nearly dead silence as the last of the thousands enter deeper water. In the darkness of night all that can be heard is labored breathing and the occasional baying of some of the younger animals, frightened by their first experience of near weightlessness. Having no firm purchase beneath their hooves is a foreign feeling, but they simply follow, doing as the rest of the herd does. This long twilight swim will be a valuable lesson to those younger ones, although there is no strong current like exists in the dangerous rivers ahead.

From his position in the rear third of the vast swimming mass of animals, the great bull can see only bobbing heads and antlers surrounding him. The darkness of night has taken the valley, but a single bright light is visible at a great distance to the left, far across the body of water. The strange light is ignored by all as they continue the crossing of the lake. They swim on for nearly forty minutes.

On the far shore the leaders are emerging from the water. After vigorously shaking to remove the excess weight, they plod on, through the ring of alders to the relatively smooth tundra above. Here they will rest the herd and gather strength and nourishment for the days of travel ahead.

The great old bull, having dragged himself up the bluff, is winded from the long swim. The years weigh heavy. There was a time when the exertion of the journey was a mere afterthought, but now, at his advanced age, the bull questions his ability to keep up the feverish pace to the mating ground. He meanders toward a shallow gully where he intends to rest for most of the night.

But it won't be long before the herd will be moving again...

The scent is heavy. And it's close.

The predator creeps forward in the dark, remaining out of sight and downwind of the advancing herd. Nearly one hundred twenty pounds of ferocious muscle and energy crouch cocked like compressed spring steel, waiting for the perfect, opportune moment to pounce. The distance to the prey is only forty yards, and the musky scent fills the nostrils of the fierce leader of the resident pack of the valley of the lake. She waits patiently for the others to reach their ambush points.

Her hair is coal-black with intermingled gray and silver. Hot breath escapes her partially opened mouth to the cool night air as the moment nears. Steely yellow eyes pierce the darkness, selecting the most vulnerable of the herd. A large male is selected.

The caribou had come ashore not far from her dug-out burrow, alerting the pack with the splashing of water as they waded to the rocky shore. Although nearly a pitch-dark night, she saw with perfect clarity that they were worn down from the long swim. They sat silently, waiting for a signal from the pack leader. She bolted toward the dry stream gullies downwind of the great mass of caribou, and the seven adults of the pack followed closely behind. *"What easy pickins,"* she thought.

This has been a very productive valley. The resident pack of wolves has ambushed caribou near this spot on many occasions over the last eight years. They lay in wait as the prey closes the distance to an unknown kill site, then strike the weakest of the herd. Usually, the kill is made quickly, the vulnerable throat of the unlucky caribou ripped out with one clench and twist of powerful jaws. Of course it doesn't always turn out as perfectly as it sounds.

Once, as a much younger and less experienced member of the pack, she was nearly trampled by a young bull caribou when an improperly calculated leap for the throat yielded only an ear. The bull was nearly brought to the ground, but struck out with a hoof, thumping the young she-wolf sharply in the ribs. The very fortunate bull ran to join the herd as she recovered her wind. Yes, the bulls are often more dangerous than the cows, and are usually avoided unless injured or obviously easy prey.

Fortunately, another, more skilled wolf of the pack managed to bring down two large cows, providing nourishment for all of the pack. A young calf returned to find what had become of her mother, and they devoured the young one as well, allowing the youngest of the pack to make the kill.

Life for all is full of such lessons, whether you are travelling through, or hunting in, the valley of the lake.

* * *

The great bull rests in the gully with his legs tucked beneath his massive belly. Soon, he should rise to graze a bit – to gather nourishment for the remainder of the trip. The desire to rest is stronger now than the desire to eat. That's not a very desirable state, given that caribou are perpetual foragers, resting only to digest the most recent meal.

But everything is not right on this cloudy, dark night.

The bull hears a rustle off to his right and with that, he realizes that he should not be this far from the main part of the herd. But it's too late. The rustling reveals a shadow, and the shadow becomes a charging wolf – ears laid back and running low to the ground.

The bull struggles to rise to his feet, but is slammed in the side of the head by the full-on charge of the large, black she-wolf. Her long canine teeth bury deep in the neck of the great bull, initially not a killing grip, but she quickly changes her grip to clasp his throat firmly in her powerful jaws. The bull is lying on his left side, having been bowled over by the impact of the wolf. He strikes with his right forefoot, but the wolf twists sharply to avoid his kick, ripping his jugular vein and tearing his windpipe. Just then, another impact – to his belly – and there is a burning sensation as a second wolf rips his belly open.

The bull still has his vision, and can see caribou running by him in the dark. He can see the steely dark eyes of the wolf as she clenches tighter to get a better grip on his tender throat. He feels her hot breath on him, and hears the low, hungry growl as she holds him, urging him to expire.

He obliges, and the pack of wolves renders the once great bull to a pile of stripped bones and torn hide in the matter of an hour.

High fog blankets the Nishlik lake valley as the hunters emerge from their shelters. A hasty breakfast is prepared of dry cereal and granola before gearing up for a day of hunting caribou.

The hunters pair up and move out over the gravel bar to an obvious trail leading to the tundra above the lake. Lungs burn from the initial climb, which is near vertical for the first few hundred yards.

"Wow, did you hear those wolves howling last night around eleven or so?" asks one hunter as he pants to catch his breath.

"It was really eerie, wasn't it...? They were certainly excited about something," answers his buddy.

"Maybe we'll get a shot at one this week. I would really love to take home a wolf hide, but they say you can't really hunt them, because they're just too wary."

"They know we're here, and will probably move out of the area to keep us from even getting a glimpse of them, but damn, you're right, it sure would be nice to get a crack at one."

As the two hunters top out on the tundra above the lake, they spot at least a couple dozen seagulls and ravens off in a gully about three hundred yards distant. One hunter glasses the group of birds, noticing that they are gathered in not one, but four areas within the gully and are hopping and flapping about in what appears to be an excited fashion.

"They're feeding on something, I can see bones scattered here and there. Let's go check it out."

The hunters are walking over spongy tussocks covered with patches of ripe blueberries broken by areas of smooth, gray-colored moss and lichen. The walking is very good, as walking in Alaska goes, and then it gets much better.

At the top of one of the many mounds that roll gently over the entire length of the valley, they walk upon what appear to be cattle trails – many of them. The trails run as far as they can see over the tundra from one far end of the valley, through it, and then converge at a low pass to the north. The trails rise and dip with the lay of the terrain, sometimes criss-crossing, sometimes running parallel, but always running in the same general direction. There were literally hundreds of trails embedded in the earth before them.

"My God... how many caribou would it take to make a trail system like that?"

"There must be thousands and thousands of caribou moving through this area, but where the hell are they? We haven't seen anything stirring except those birds."

"Let's keep going to see what those birds are so excited about."

Long moments later, the two hunters top the last rise between them and the scene of carnage that has captured the attention of the ravens and seagulls, which take flight at the approach of the two intruders. There before them are the carcasses of four caribou, three of which are bulls – very large bulls judging from the size of the antlers that lay attached to bright pink dismembered skeletons. There was hair, hide, blood, bones and viscera scattered over the entire gully. There had been a major feast here, but not by the two-legged predators who stand in awe and wonder at the scene.

After taking a picture of the killing ground, the two hunters removed the antlers from the carcasses of the three bulls, and attached them to pack frames for the walk back toward the camp. The antlers were massive, and reached high above and forward of their bodies.

Later that evening, at the hunting camp, the four hunters share the day's experiences. The scene of the four slaughtered caribou being described in detail, as the hunters pored over the trophy caribou antlers recovered without the firing of even one shot.

The other pair of hunters had not traveled far from camp, choosing a ridge that provided a good vantage point over the entire valley. Anything that moved for miles around could be spotted, but only the movement of the opposing hunters was noted.

There were only the trails left by the thousands of caribou that covered the valley on the night before – the thousands that escaped the jaws of the hungry residents of the valley.

But the hunting week was young, and there would be many shooting opportunities before the Otter arrived to carry the four hunters back to their lives and families. The two-legged hunters would create their own individual killing fields, and everlasting memories, as stragglers to the herd would filter through the valley of the lake in hopes of catching up to the main herd – the herd of thousands... that got away.

The black she-wolf stands outside her burrow scanning the valley floor for movement on a misty, dreary day in the valley.

A large bird lands quietly at the far end of the lake, and then departs with a buzzing sound, circling once before climbing away, into the clouds. She waits patiently for the next herd to pass.

The herd of thousands is growing bigger still, as three smaller bands of caribou have joined the main body of animals since the crossing of the lake. The matriarch pushes across a large river, and nearly the entire herd remains intact. She and the other adults have succeeded at imparting upon the younger members the necessity to keep moving at all cost toward the wintering grounds.

As they pause on a misty afternoon, she hears the sound of the thunder sticks carried by the two-legged predator. She quickly gets the herd moving again toward safer pastures. Their movement is perpetual, as it has been for thousands of years.

Sealing the Deal

Nervous; he just can't shake the jitters that accompany the moment before the shot.   Adrenaline flows freely through his veins, although the large male black bear approaching through the spruce forest comes mostly expected.   That doesn't change the nervous excitement that causes his palms to sweat, and his bow to shake in his hands as he places the release on the loop to the rear of the string.   He has been sitting in this stand for each of the last three evenings, and is now hoping that fate will finally allow the bear who has been raiding the bait station just after dark to break his routine.

Well the bear's routine has been broken, but the hunter's anxious routine persists.   He recalls the first time.   In the oak-studded piney woods of Mississippi, when the whitetail deer buck cautiously approached the thirteen-year-old hunter's tree stand at the edge of the soybean field.   A tiny heart pounded with anticipation. A cold shiver reverberated through the young body. Anticipation of what... the shot? Anticipation of the kill? Maybe it was being in the presence of a game animal – and its absence of the knowledge of the young hunter's lethal posture above that gave him the strange feeling that he experiences to this day, each time he is poised to send the target of his passions - his desires -

to its final destination; the eternal memory of the hunter.

Then, it was a .410 gauge shotgun with a lead slug. Now it is a compound bow and carbon arrows tipped with razor-sharp blades of steel. He has evolved through a series of tools of the trade, each providing a measure of lethality appropriate to the quarry and the conditions of the hunt. Through the changes, some things remain the same. Years and months of practice culminate in a single moment for those who participate in this deadly game, but for him, the nervous excitement that may sometimes accompany the shot is ever-present. And this time it is especially bad.

If I miss, the bear may very well turn on me, he thinks.

The large black mass stirs beneath the dense alder and willow cover. The source of heat and light hangs lower in the daylight sky, and a cool breeze awakens the bear from restful sleep. He lets out a long yawn and rolls up on his haunches, appearing much like a plump black ball of hair below beady, sleepy eyes.

Travelling mostly in the evening and night, he evades the mid-day warmth. It is a constant search for food to nourish his massive body, and he will eat nearly everything that presents itself. Tender shoots of greens are widely available, but flesh is what he craves; and he has found a plentiful supply of it nearby. It's never been this easy, and the scent of the rotten flesh lingers on his jutting brown snout and large paws.

The smell first captured his attention three nights ago as he trailed the young calves of a moose. They were just ahead of him, but across a large bog, and the going would be difficult. In spite of his strong desire to taste the tender flesh of the newborns, they were now running headlong away from him across the spongy terrain, the long legs of the mother leading them to the safety that only distance from him can provide...

And there it was, the strong, fetid scent of rotten flesh. He turned directly and approached cautiously the source of the smell, checking the wind constantly for any contenders who may have already found the rather obvious feast.

Of course, there were none, and he gorged himself for nearly an hour before collapsing nearby for a long, deep, nap.

His belly was now rumbling for the taste, and he was beginning to salivate in anticipation of the now familiar meal. Rolling forward he launched himself onto all fours, instinctively oriented in the direction of the strange, cylindrical object of his immediate desire.

The previous fall the hunter was in position to harvest a tremendous caribou bull. While waiting patiently in his stand, his thoughts drift to that hunt, and how his torment nearly ruined the shot.

Having spotted three bulls as they bedded for the afternoon, but a full mile away, he planned a stalk that would take him to a stream drainage just downwind of their position. The closer he got the more adrenaline his heart received, which caused him to

sweat in the fall coolness.   As he closed to within shooting distance and could see the antlers of the largest of the three bulls just over the horizon, he froze. The beat of his heart could be felt within his ears as if listening though a stethoscope.   Creeping forward, he placed the crosshairs of the 6X scope on the horizon and walked forward. The back of the bull slowly filled the bottom of the scope from the distance that had been closed to a mere thirty yards. An ear flickered. The bull stood, exposing an entire right flank to the hunter with the full scope. But the crosshairs would not cease their fluttering.   The thin hairs of the reticle passed behind the shoulder and he jerked the trigger, causing the barrel of the rifle to lower. The last thing he saw in his scope was the daylight between the bull's legs... and that is precisely where the bullet passed.

He recovered quickly, instinctively chambering another round into the rifle. The bull bounded forward, front legs leaving the ground in a high arc, then he was off running. The other bulls leapt up and followed. At seventy yards, the bulls paused and looked back. The hunter shot again and finally closed the deal. Lucky breaks are dealt with random imprecision, but he was fortunate enough to be on the receiving end of at least this one.

"I must learn to control these emotions." He remembers saying aloud, apparently to no one. Or maybe he was speaking to the two remaining bulls who were loping away only on the fortune of having lesser antlers than their traveling companion.

Of course the story of the hunt told at camp that night did not include the trajectory of the first misplaced bullet, or the cold sweat that the hunter broke out in before the shot. Yep, it was a secret condition; suffered in silence, and in his case, the diagnosis was "terminal."

Now, as he studies the distant approach of the bear who has haunted his dreams for the past two nights, he strains to capture the reason for his anxiety once the fine line is crossed; when a creature is no longer being viewed, but is now being hunted. The deep thought is entered into as a diversion from the reality that his world is about to again be overtaken by adrenaline and its effect on his nerves.

Is it wrong for me to feel this way? What if this is nature's way of telling me that I am not suited for the deadly task of pursuit and capture...? My desires are for the hunt, the hunting seasons, and the feeling of elation that I get when I am ultimately successful, but what of this state that acts as a barrier to my fulfillment? It has caused me to miss opportunities before, but surely the animal that I pursue is not subconsciously asking of me not to take the shot. I've got to learn to detach myself from the act of killing, even though I am about to quite possibly cause the heart of the beast to cease – draining his memories, desires, and instincts. That's it. I'll pretend that it is not a moving, breathing animal, but just a paper target. It's just like the 3-D targets that I have shot thousands of times before...

Moist black nostrils taste the air, searching for the scent of another bear. His massive brown snout turns left and right, allowing his limited eyesight to aid in the location of any threat to his enjoying another bellyful of the rotten beaver carcass that has been strangely trapped within the large metal object. His belly grumbles, much like when he approaches a defenseless new moose calf. His eager anticipation of the first taste of blood makes his mouth lather with saliva, and he can hardly control the urge to rip forward, possibly alerting the prey. His front paws, with ebony claws protruding forward, claw the ground with each extended step. He woofs loudly with excitement, but also to alert all who may hear that the ruler of this bog, and this newfound food source, is near.

The hunter snaps out of his daydreaming state as the bark of the bear pierces the air. It is not a particularly terrifying sound, unless heard while alone in the wild, where there is no immediate escape or any appeasement that may be offered the maker of the sound that will remove the agitation or excitement – except to shoot or leave. The shooter slowly lowers his head to check that his arrow is properly knocked. He pulls back with his right elbow to test the caliper release against the string. He feels pressure there, so backs off. It's not time yet. *I'm going to watch this animal until I stop shaking and then I am never going to allow this to happen again.*

He examines the bear inch by inch from the mere twenty yards that separate him from the boar. It's the largest black bear he has ever seen, in picture or in real life. His head is massive and round, giving his ears a very small, seemingly insignificant appearance. He is jet-black, with velvety, long hair characteristic of the bears known to frequent this large swamp to the north and west of Anchorage, Alaska. The short brown hairs of his muzzle are turning gray near the front of his snout, showing his advanced age.

With one paw, his left, he reaches through the hole in the barrel to remove a large wad of stinky, gooey, rotten beaver flesh and bone. It falls to the ground and the bear wastes no time in devouring it. He plops back onto his haunches, providing the hunter a visual reference as to his size. His shoulders are higher than the top of the fifty-five gallon drum, and he is at least as big around.

This bear must weigh in excess of four hundred pounds, the hunter exclaims to himself in silence.

Those thoughts only add to the excitement, and now he is quivering with anticipation. Funny, the night before, a small sow with a cub visited the barrel just before dark, and as soon as the bear was identified as having a cub, making it illegal to shoot, he was able to watch it and the cub at this short distance without the nervous jitters that he feels now. *It must be the shot that makes me nervous. The thought that this animal can be mine if I can just steady a sight pin over his vitals and control the release of the arrow. If I'm watching, there's no problem, but if I am aware that a shot may present itself, I begin to fall apart... Okay, it's just a 3-D target, remember.*

Well, the "3-D target" reaches in for another helping of the putrid slop that had been gathered in the previous winter trapping season. Each beaver was skinned, then cut into quarters and stored in five gallon buckets, with the addition of warm grease of the fryer of a restaurant run by a friend. The contents of the bucket decay through the winter and into spring, becoming the dream attractant and center-of-the-barrel entrée that will draw a bear for miles around. The neat, closed-lid pickle buckets, also supplied by the restaurant owner, contain the smell and make for easy transport to the bait site, one or two at a time, as needed, during nightly and weekly outings to the site before and during the season.

Without the use of a bait station, hunting black bears in this area, and in most of Alaska for that matter, would be by chance contact only. Many fewer bears would be taken, and their omnivorous nature would greatly reduce the numbers of moose calves that survive the first year, which is the most critical aspect supporting their ability to reach maturity. He knows that we are all predators, to some extent, but when some predators begin to tip the balance unfavorably, then that predator must be regulated. Hence, one hunter perched seventeen feet above and twenty-three yards from a barrel of bait.

The hunter stands on the tiny platform, which is affixed to the large spruce tree with a nylon strap and self-locking buckle. His left foot is forward, toward the barrel, and his bow is held in his left hand. Evening light is fading, and it is necessary to get on with the business of sending a carbon, razor-tipped arrow toward the chest of this magnificent animal. Excuse me... "3-D target" of a large black bear.

The bear is fixated on the slop that lies before him, so the hunter raises the bow until the sight bracket and forward stabilizer are near level with his eyes. This is the point of no return. Once the muscles are contracted and leverage is utilized drawing the string to the rear, there will be no turning back. To let off would be to immediately frighten the bear from the area with the excessive movement that it would cause. He crosses the demarcation line by flexing the muscles of his upper back, and the string, held by the mechanical release, creeps rearward, rolling the large cams holding it until the bow buckles toward him in a carefully tuned series of angles, limbs, and cables that scream with kinetic energy. The pencil-thin carbon arrow slid to the rear effortlessly, and now stands cocked on its rest. Once released, it will explode forward with minimal vibration or flexation, piercing the air at nearly three hundred fifty feet per second. It will reach the target, at this distance, in one-fifth of a second.

He stands rigid, muscles taut, as the formed-foam 3-D target of a black bear reaches toward the barrel with his right hand this time, exposing the area behind his shoulder to the chiseled tip of the broadhead that is directed toward it. A fluorescent green dot hovers over the area, viewed by the archer through a plastic ring entwined into the string. *Dead bear,* flashes through the mind of the hunter as the air is pierced by the arrow as it is launched toward the large dark shape with its leg outstretched toward the barrel.

* * *

The bear feels nothing more than a stinging as the razor blades pass through its chest. First on the right, then instantaneously on the left as the arrow travels completely through his body. His reflexes react more to the crash of the arrow into the brush on his left than to its passing through his lungs. He wheels to his right, springing away from the barrel, snapping with his teeth at the bees that sting him from both sides of his chest. The dying bruin runs for little more than three seconds, but has covered nearly thirty yards in that time before barreling into the lower limbs of a large spruce tree. He has no breath, and strangely, cannot inhale, although his lungs burn for air. He collapses as the blood ceases its travel to his brain, instead pooling within his chest as it spurts from his pierced lungs. He attempts to moan, but only gurgles as blood spews forth from his mouth and nose. The forest floor is visible before his eyes, but it is at an odd angle that he is not familiar with. He attempts to right his head, but cannot lift it. A cold chill washes over him, and the forest floor is now black as he drifts, tingling, weightlessly, toward the limbs above.

It was over in mere seconds, and the last thing the archer saw was the fletch of his arrow, bright pink, against the black of the bear's chest. Then the bear bolted to the right and crashed, out of sight. The hunter hears him gurgling, attempting a moan, as if to notify all that might hear that the forest is now safe from his menacing. He had heard that death moan before, and is thankful that he is spared from its horrible, spooky sound.

The hunter begins to shake in earnest, and needs to steady himself against the tree to keep from falling out of the stand. A tremendous wave of happiness washes over him, as if he has completed a long journey and can finally rest. He collapses into the seat of the stand and relives the shot over and over.

It is dark now, just twenty minutes later, so he digs a headlamp from his daypack and illuminates the area in front of his face. He has heard no movement on the part of the bear since it crashed into the tree, so he decides that it is okay to climb down the stand's ladder toward the ground.

Just fifteen yards away lay the large black bear, appearing to be a shadow against the spongy floor of the stand of spruce. He walks over to it, and again begins to shake violently. He has once more "closed the deal", and is overcome by the feeling of something being given to him, and yet having a sense of tremendous loss at the same time.

The moment finally passes, and he now digs for his skinning knife that is at the bottom of his pack.

I think I'll skin this one for a life-sized mount, was his first thought as he made his first incision near the tail of the bear, the passing torment of excited energy having subsided for now.

-- "The deal" is this; you are offered the opportunity to end the life of one of nature's more beautiful creatures. In return, you promise to hold his living memory sacred among your most valuable possessions, passing the details of his taking down throughout the generations, and speaking of him as if he were the most incredible creature that ever existed. – Marc

Breathless, Under the Weight
Of a Hunter's Moment

Motionless. Breathless.   The hunter stands watching as the bull's head turns slowly in his direction. The subtle movement of a bowstring to its taut, lethal and drawn position has alerted the great beast to a foreign presence. The bull's chest heaves with each breath; nostrils seeking to catch the scent of the intruder. The hunter's muscles begin to strain and twitch as he searches for the proper shooting window, free of obstruction, which will allow the arrow to reach its intended mark.

Months of preparation on behalf of the hunter have led to this single tense moment. The imitated calls of a bull moose have deceived this bull into thinking that its maker is a worthy adversary. The challenge issued, he came to this location in search of a fight; a fight that occasionally results in death to the weaker opponent. Such a bull moose as this, so regal, so advanced in his age has survived many such confrontations.

The hunter now focuses his energy through the sight, onto the pin that will represent the strike of the broadhead.

The bull can sense a presence; his gaze is seeking the familiar movements of a challenging bull that he is prepared to fight; his huge eyes are searching. Ears are pivoting. He is yearning to pick up the familiar sound and sight of an approaching challenger.

His eyes lock onto *you.*

He is broadside; one massive right antler reaches beyond the hump in his back as he stares intently, yet questioningly, at the unfamiliar shape before him.

Surely this is not the rival who has captured my attention from afar, He thinks. *Certainly this puny, upright creature is no permanent threat to the reign of such a regal patriarch of the Alaska tundra.*

The fingers of the hunter's shooting hand relax as the sight pin rests on its mark. The arrow leaves the bow with the sound of a whisper.

A piercing pain penetrates the ribcage of the great bull. He whirls his huge body in a powerfully reflexive turn. The frail looking upright creature has been underestimated, and has cast a blow from a distance. The bull assumes a fighting posture as a strange warmth fills his chest. The warmth is soon replaced by a chill that creeps slowly to his back and shoulders as his vision of the puny foe becomes unfocused.

Massive legs that have carried his huge body high above his familiar terrain now strain to hold his weight. He lunges forward, but his legs do not respond, causing the once mighty bull moose to collapse forward.

You experience the feeling of watching from a distance as these precious moments pass like slow-motion frames in a vivid dream.

The hunter moves quickly now to nock another arrow as the bull struggles on the ground before him. The massive chest still heaves, but not with the vigor of previous moments. As he draws the bowstring again, the bull utters a cough, then a sigh and rests the weight of his head and neck upon one massive antler. A long, final breath escapes his now bloodied nostrils; his chest becomes motionless – *breathless* – as the second arrow is buried within him.

You realize that you are no longer the observer in this fatal moment. You are the hunter...

You creep forward cautiously, expecting what is no longer possible, having reduced to possession one of the grandest of creatures to ever have walked the earth.

The chill washes over *the hunter* now, seeping through your chest to your shoulders and finally, to trembling hands. Your vision is blurred as well, but with the tears that fill your eyes. You stand in admiration of what your efforts have produced. In wonder – that you have allowed yourself to cause the death of such a beautiful animal - one as evolved within its environment as we are within our own.

You ask forgiveness, seeking affirmation that your reasons to commit such an act are honorable.

Now kneeling, face buried in your hands, you are again breathless. And the weight of this dream-like moment comes to rest upon your shoulders.

-- *When asking the hunting gods to provide a moment such as this, be fully aware that the desired outcome is the death of another being. Once the string is released, or the trigger is pulled, there is no recall of that deadly action. Your "moment" will continue, and the moment of the hunted will cease. Commit his memory to dwell among your most treasured possessions. – Marc*

The View From An Aspen Grove

Dazed and confused.

The great brown bear emerges from the snow pack to blinding sunlight. He has rested in deep slumber for more than five months. Ropey muscles are stiff from the lack of physical exertion that the replenishing sleep demands.

The area that this old boar chose in the late fall for his den looks much different now through sleep-glazed eyes, and many feet of snow have fallen since he scraped out the shallow cave late in October of the previous year. The leafless tips of alders and shadows of gray rocks are the only contrasts to the blinding white snow – with the exception of a brilliant blue sky.

This is the thirteenth time that he has clawed toward the faint light high above his bed of willow and alder branches. Some winters, when not much snow falls the initial clawing is no great matter, but this year it seemed to take forever to finally break free; the wind having blown an additional fifteen feet of snow over his dormant domain. The great bear collapses near the opening and his dark brown mass absorbs the warmth of the spring sunshine. He will lie still for nearly three hours before gathering himself and his senses. The sleep is necessary and rejuvenating, yet so exhausting at the same time.

The very large and right now very sleep-drunk brown bear ambles toward a small grove of aspen trees protruding from the endless sea of snow. The reasons behind the interest they hold are simple enough. The grove is the only recognizable feature on this pure – painfully pure – cloud of white; and the rumbling deep within his stomach reminds him that there is unfinished business somewhere below those branches.

The air is crisp on this April morning in the mountains of the western Alaska Range. No. Razor sharp. The air is razor sharp upon exposed flesh. The drowsy hunter offers thanks to the sleeping bag god for the *"Wiggy" sleeping bag* that separates him from the bitter cold. With mere inches between his scantily clad body and the freezing bite of the mountain air, he lies deep within the comfort of his warm, safe, mummy-like environment. He had been dreaming of being wrapped in the warmth of his beautiful wife's arms, and longing for the welcoming embrace that he will receive upon his triumphant return from the hunting grounds. The reception is always the same, for love afforded a hunter by a loving spouse does not hinge on the success of the hunt. Wives of hunters would wager that their man's thoughts could never drift in a homeward direction within the duration of the hunt; but oh, how sadly mistaken they are.

The younger of the two hunters widens the cinched breathing hole above his nose, and calls to wake his hunting companion in an adjacent tent. Frosty breath spews forth from the opening, drifting momentarily before freezing to the sides of the tent. The two hunters were flown by airplane into the nearby frozen lake, affording each his separate quarters. This is a luxury not known to the hunters who have to travel overland on foot to reach their destination.

An overnight glacial zephyr, blowing at regular intervals through the clear and terribly cold night has dumped driven snow – more than two feet of it – around the lower half of the young hunter's tent, so there was not much sleep to be had by either hunter. Their nerves were worn thin by the fierce wind and blowing snow that howled through the night. It would be dead silent for a number of seconds, and then you could hear the zephyr approaching. *Ssshheeeeeeeeww.*

The tents would shake violently for fifteen or twenty seconds until the next lull, which began as abruptly as the winds. The hunters were never in any real danger, it's just unnerving when accustomed to sleeping in the comfort of your quiet bedroom for most of the year, with slumber disturbed only by the rude, intrusive buzzing or ringing of the morning's alarm clock.

Predawn light will reveal only one thing to the hunters as they emerge from their fragile dwellings: White. Everything is pure white, with the exception of a purple sky, which will turn bright blue as the sun peeks above the horizon. The temperature is too low to ponder. A breakfast of hot cereal will be necessary in order to rekindle the fire of warmth that sputters within as they climb from the cold shelter. A fire is quickly struck utilizing the latest in combustion technology – and there you have it, instant warmth in the form of boiling water and a pre-made instant oatmeal mixture.

It won't be a very distant trek to the hunting pit dug from the snow into the side of a mountain. From the vantage point, the hunters will overlook a wide, rolling valley. The pit which shields them from the wind and masks their subtle movements and stirrings must be somewhat comfortable as hunting for spring brown bear is dreadfully uneventful, usually entailing endless hours of waiting.

The pair push toward their ambush site on webbed snowshoes. It would be impossible to travel in the deep snow without spreading the weight of a body over a larger area. They drag a near-empty sled made of sturdy plastic, which will aid in the removal of a very heavy bear hide in the event that this year – as opposed to the previous two – the hunters are fortunate enough to get a shot at the large old boar that makes this valley his home during the late fall.

These particular hunters have shared many of the priceless moments that are known to those who venture away from the beaten path. They are alone, again, in a pure white springtime world, far from the comforts they so willingly leave behind in their search for the everlasting hunter's moment.

There must be fifteen or twenty feet of snow covering everything in this valley, save a lonely stand of trees below the hunters at a distance of nearly four hundred yards. To come back to this very spot in mid-summer, the same hunters would be lost, as the landscape would resemble nothing of its current state. The relatively warm waters of a distant inlet assure ample winter snow to this range of mountains.

* * *

It is nearly two miles from the bear's den to the stand of leafless aspens. A rocky stream meanders through the trees, but it is under many feet of snow like everything else in this land. Months before, the trees were witness to a brutal fight between an old, nearly toothless moose and a very large, deep-chocolate colored brown bear. Of course there was not much of a fight on behalf of the moose, so maybe it was more like a killing...

The bull moose attempted to flee from the brown bear that it happened upon, with misfortune, while grazing on native willows near the stream. The bear attacked the bull from a flank and quickly grasped its neck in powerful jaws, digging in with nearly four-inch claws to maintain a firm hold. Two beasts, weighing in excess of twelve hundred pounds each – one a relatively docile and meandering herbivore, the other a fierce and territorial omnivore – wrestled briefly as life slowly escaped the antlered of the two.

With such powerful jaws and razor-sharp claws, any creature in possession of them would feel invincible in this land.

This particular stand of trees had served as witness to happenings such as these on many occasions during its half-century of growth; the goings and comings of thousands of animals, large and small, passing beneath their boughs. Being the tallest growth in the valley, animals are drawn to investigate their shade with premeditation, as one might be drawn toward an oasis in a dry desert. The eye sees many individual trees, but aspens are actually one root system, with many shoots growing from the single sprawling, dominating stem. The ground-stingy aspen chokes out most foreign growth making way for future trunks to thrive from its roots. Usually where you see aspens growing, that's all that you see are aspens.

The unfortunate moose, unknowingly occupying his presupposed place in the circle of life and death, was quickly covered with leaves which had begun to fall from the deciduous trees. Mossy ground was excavated from near the carcass in the big boar's attempt to conceal and claim it for future use. The trapped heat would speed decay, allowing natural enzymes and bacteria to tenderize the flesh, readying it for the bear's consumption. As life to the naked eye ceases, it in turn spurns equally complex life forms that begin to dispose of the visible reminders in their microscopic, yet so destructive way.

The bear's last act before leaving the area was to urinate on the heap, identifying it as belonging to him. Soon, the snows began to fall, further concealing the fallen moose from predators. The kill would come in very handy once the dormant time was completed, and the bear would return to this exact spot upon his awakening – to reclaim his prize.

The hunters each possess a large-caliber .375 H&H Magnum rifle, known for its lethal ability to bring down even the most dangerous of North-American animals. The projectiles they have chosen are the heaviest available for the caliber, and at their weight of 300 grains, will deliver punishing penetration and destructive energy upon impact.

With this rifle and bullet combination at his disposal, any hunter in its possession would feel invincible in this land.

They reached their dugout in the side of the mountain to find it had been half-filled with blown snow. The two hunters take turns digging the freshly-blown snow out utilizing their snowshoes as shovels. The labor is not particularly tiresome, and they are careful not to cause overheating beneath their bulky winter clothes. To perspire in the extreme cold is to invite chill into your body, and that must be avoided with forethought for each activity undertaken.

Gear is stored within easy reach and the sled used as a seat to prevent the hunters from sitting directly on the snow. All in all, this is a very comfortable, if not cozy, little place to ambush a great bear. Only their heads protrude from the pit, and from a distance must have looked like two rocks jutting from deep within the snow.

Through polarized sunglasses the hunters immediately begin scanning the bright snow-scape as if someone had given the command, "Go!", and the hunt was on again.

Saliva is slow in returning to the bear's parched mouth. It has been nearly five months since flesh or water have passed across his tongue, so he bites at the snow to moisten his dry throat. Four massive paws disperse his weight, allowing him to negotiate the deep white powder with nominal effort. His eyes are slowly becoming adjusted to the bright light of day as he makes his way carefully toward the blurry image that has captured his attention.

The sustained motion of his short jaunt is welcoming to his stiff, powerful body. Although his heart still beats at a near comatose level, blood is flowing at a much more rapid rate than the depths sustained during his long sleep. Unbeknownst to him during sleep, his muscles shivered and contracted involuntarily to refrain from atrophy to a point that would be counter-productive upon his awakening. He remains strong, but his muscle-memory-motion is lost, therefore he must relearn the fluid swagger that he possessed in the previous fall.

It is great to be alive, even on such a cold spring day; and the days will be lengthening, bringing with them the promise of lush green surroundings and rivers that will flow full with salmon again. Although he is a solitary creature, he looks forward to the confrontations and chance encounters that will take place in the summer ahead. The great boar can hardly wait to again assert his dominance over this, his home range.

He stops on a small shelf in the mountain, not more than a mile from the den that he so eagerly escaped earlier this morning. Sipping the air around him, he detects a foreign scent that he does not recognize from the previous year's travels.

They have watched for only an hour and a half, already the elder of the two hunters is drifting off to shallow sleep, trying to reclaim some of the rest lost during the previous night's wind storm. The younger hunter is more alert, realizing that if they both nap, the large bear they are pursuing could be lucky enough to wander into and out of sight right under their closed eyes.

To keep himself entertained, the younger hunter rehashes the events leading to this moment: The flight by Super Cub as the skis break free of the frozen lake on the other side of the inlet. The back of the pilot's head as it rotates and pivots, scanning for air traffic as they gain altitude and set a course for the narrowest part of the large icy body of water they must cross. Occasionally, the pilot would point down, indicating fresh tracks in the snow as they passed quickly beneath the low-flying plane. The tracks were numerous, but the maker was elusive in presence, always seemingly just over the next rise; but the tracks led even farther away once that point was reached. The hunter recalls how he was mesmerized by the steep mountains whizzing past on either side as the tiny plane negotiated a narrow gorge at low altitude.

Just as the passenger began to feel as though he would allow this flight to go on forever, the plane banked sharply and dove to a snow-covered mountain lake, landing in short order.

Upon arrival the hunter and the pilot made small talk about whether this will be the location that the bear passes through this year. The pilot gives his assurance that there is a large bear somewhere within five miles or so, and this place is as good a place as any for him to wander through. The veteran pilot chuckles, "That's about as good as it gets with spring bear hunting." He then prepares his plane to leave.

The first hunter and gear deposited, the plane fires up quickly and blasts off the snow-covered mountain lake. This is now as alone as a person can feel on this planet, the hunter remembers: *Standing, on a frozen lake in the middle of a frozen mountain range as the plane that brought me here climbs away from me.*

All you have at this moment is a small amount of gear, and a terrific amount of faith – that's it.

That was yesterday. The camp was prepared and the hunters moved toward the valley containing the grove of trees. They dug the pit and returned to relax at the camp, preparing a hot meal before retiring on the eve of the first day of the hunt.

For now, he is staring at an ocean of white, waiting for a large brown bear to walk to or through this valley in the middle of a frozen mountain range.

What are the odds...?

The hunter stares at a large dark spot on the sea of white. "Was that there a moment ago?" he questions.

He is speaking out loud, but to whom? His hunting partner of many years is sleeping like a baby next to him. A strong nudge brings the older hunter back to reality, and he is startled by the sudden end to his short nap.

The odor is remotely familiar to the old boar. It is the faint scent of the upright creature, of which he has only seen on three occasions. On the last occasion, the boar was nearing a useful fishing hole late in the summer of last year. He happened upon two of the upright creatures standing on a bank near the river. They acted very surprised to see the old boar approaching from above them. The two quickly crossed the fast-running stream and walked away from him on the other side of it. The bear did not attempt to pursue them because of the acrid smell that followed them. Instead, he settled in at the river to gorge himself on the late run of bright silver salmon. The upright creatures returned in time, and there was a terrific noise. A large stone at the bear's feet exploded, pelting the bear in the face with shattered rock. The noise was very startling to the bear, so he escaped to the alders and watched as the upright creatures crossed back to his side of the stream to gawk at the tracks he had left behind. On that occasion the bear retreated to the safety of thick cover. *This time, the upright creatures would not be so fortunate if they make an attempt to keep him from what lies at the foot of the grove of trees.*

The smell was not nearly as strong as the last time he encountered it, so the bear continued toward the stand of trees.

He lumbers along, not overexerting his tired body. The route of travel carried him downhill at an angle. Soon he will reach the bottom of the slope and then it will be level, near where a small creek winds through the valley in the summer.

"Here comes your bear!"

"Where...What?"

"There, he's coming downhill in our direction. He's a huge boar. Beautiful. Dark brown."

Of the three hearts in this valley, two of them were beating furiously. Released adrenalin was causing thoughts to race and respiration to quicken in the two excited hunters. They have sat patiently in this valley for one week in the spring of the two preceding years and have not seen movement other than passing ravens, and on one occasion a wolverine scurrying through.

This trip was already very different.

The younger hunter had the bear centered in his binoculars, and was trying to absorb every detail of the bear at the distance of a little over a mile – but the behemoth was closing the distance at a rapid rate.

In his excitement, the older hunter, who would be the shooter, ejected the chambered round – intended to be the first one fired, into the snow. It was retrieved and fed into the throat of the rifle; the bolt closed with a sound of steel contacting steel as the locking lugs engaged the steel rings within the receiver. The rubber scope cover was removed and the hunter cranked the scope's magnification up to its highest mark. The intense wait was on for the bear to move to within range.

The odor of the upright creature was carried away by the stinging breeze that now drifted up from the lower end of the valley. With it went all thought of danger associated with the smell. The bear's focus returned to the meal that waited amid the trees. He had painstakingly hidden the carcass, and had properly marked it for all to know that it was the property of the great boar of the range. Surely it would be exactly as it had been left.

That, for the most part, was not going to be true. A pack of thirteen wolves found the cache of meat just days after the struggle for life on the part of the moose. The scent of the bear was not enough to deter the hungry pack, so they feasted on the moose – although very cautiously at first. There was nothing left for the bear but skin and hair, but he had no knowledge of the pilferage as he approached. He is now within a hundred yards of the spot where the carcass should have been lying frozen.

The bear begins to salivate at the thought of it.

The large caliber rifle rests on a day-pack, which in turn rests on a berm of snow in front of the dugout. The elder hunter concentrates on keeping the bear quartered in the scope as it walks from right to left in the man's field of vision. They have estimated the distance to the bear to be four hundred yards. In actuality, the bear is approaching a tree that is exactly three hundred and forty yards from the hunters. Their attempt to gain an accurate distance was stymied due to a laser rangefinder's inability to function in the extreme cold. If the hunters had taken the time to store the batteries for the rangefinder near the heat of their warm bodies, they would have acquired an accurate reading. But as it turns out, the end result will be the same.

The hunters watch as the bear slows his pace, with his muzzle to the ground, trying to pull the scent of the moose through the snow.

"You will need to aim high. Put your crosshair on the hump of his back – at this distance, the round will drop right into his 'boiler-room'."

"I hate holding-over. Shouldn't we just wait to see if he comes any closer?"

"No, we have to shoot soon; if he winds us he'll leave this valley like a rocket. But wait till he stops, okay."

"Okay."

The safety is purposely pushed forward to the shooting position. The shooter is shivering, partly from the cold, but mostly due to his muscles' inability to utilize the abundance of adrenalin passing through them.

"I'm shaking!"

"Man, you've *got* to nail this shot. We've been waiting for this very moment for years. Calm down. Try taking some deep breaths or something."

"Okay, that's better."

"Do you have him?"

"Yeah, right on the hump."

"Now!"

"Now what?"

"Shoot!"

The hunter's slight rearward pressure on the trigger releases the sear, which in turn releases the firing pin, causing a chain of explosions that culminate in a 300 grain Nosler bullet exiting the barrel at just over 2,600 feet per second.

He can now smell the moose. The bear pauses momentarily to scratch the ground above what is left of the moose carcass.

HHWWUUMMPPFF.........BOOOMMM

The large caliber bullet enters the bear's hide, and then explodes with 2000 pounds of pressure, pulverizing six inches of the bear's spine. He collapses onto his massive belly like a rug dropped to the floor.

The great boar can see snow in front of his face, and the bare trees above him, but otherwise, he is powerless. Such a mighty creature, reduced to a moaning mound of flesh by a piece of metal that weighs no more than an ounce. His spinal cord is severed, so he merely pants heavily – and waits. He does not understand how such a beautiful day, with so much promise, could go so wrong.

"Great shot! He dropped like the bottom fell out of the valley!"
"Should I put another one in him?"
"Not yet, let's wait and see. He fell like a ton of bricks."
The hunters grab their belongings and rush to where the bear fell... and waits.

swush...swush...swush...swush
The bear can hear them approaching, and recognizes the acrid smell, but he can not lift his head or turn to face his attackers. They suddenly appear in his peripheral vision.

"Holy cow! He's huge! You did it! You got him!"
"He's still breathing, I'm gonna put another one in him."
"Put it just behind the neck."
...BOOOMMM

A sudden wind causes the limbs of the aspens to sway gently. Its sound through the limbs is much like a mournful sigh.
The grove has witnessed yet another passing.

-- We surrender all to experience the thrill of the taking. For the hunted, there is no surrender, for they are taken without an alternative outcome being offered. Assure the hunted respect in death as well as life; for theirs is the ultimate sacrifice, and in their sacrifice we somehow achieve fulfillment... until the next surrendering, that is. – Marc

You're not alone

A Morning in a Mountain Valley Cathedral

The aging hunter awakens from broken, fitful sleep. One would think that after the many years of "opening days" it would get easier to rest on the night before the hunt. The fatigue caused by the wear and tear of the solo, steep trek into the land of the white sheep is no match for the anxious yearning to begin the hunt – even after thirty-one years spent in the pursuit of that next fulfilling experience.

As he lies still in the warmth of his sleeping bag, the old man reflects on previous trips into these rugged lands. He has hunted in every mountain range of this, the "Last Frontier" sometimes with close companions, sometimes alone, but never without reverence for the many animals has he hunted. His successes have been many. In an offering of thanks for his being welcomed again into the lofty heavens of the earth itself, he recites aloud..."*If the Lord is willing, and my aim is true, I will take a beautiful Dall ram on this day. Its flesh will nourish my body, and its memory will forever nourish my soul...*"

Some offer thanks at the end of each day for the happenstance blessings received from everyday life. A hunter of sheep asks to be blessed with success during his chosen, and often dangerous, quest.

He is surrounded by fog as he crawls out of the shelter. It is necessary to rise early in order to position himself in the path of the small band of Dall rams that feed on the steep meadows of this glacial valley.

For two days prior he has watched from a vantage point near his camp as the rams grazed down from the heights. Only the hunting gods know for sure whether they will repeat their short journey for him on this day.

A thick cloud cloaks the glacial valley as the morning twilight finds the old white ram's rocky bed. From his safe perch amid the rocks, high above the shale-guarded slopes, he awakens from intermittent sleep. The old ram stands in his bed of crushed shale and faces his mountainous domain, its ice-capped peaks and jagged, sheer faces. He has traversed nearly every foot of these mountains - his home range - having been handed down the instinct to hold the herd of sheep in his stead to an area where lush, succulent grass is less than a day's travel in most any direction.

Now in his thirteenth year, the ram is crowned with a massive set of curled horns. Etched by the years, they rise back from his head in gnarled, deep, tan splendor; their tendrils spiraling low to below his jaw before sweeping outward to pointed tips. His crown is the picture of natural, symmetrical perfection. The bone-white coat of hair has no equal in its purity or warmth, protecting the great ram from the harshest of mountain winds and cold.

This majestic old ram dwells in the heights – in the places

where only other sheep may reach, yet his solitary place is reserved for the oldest, most revered of his band. There is no other ram in this range more worthy of such a lofty, safe dwelling.

Descent from the perch begins with careful steps over the jagged rock face. With surgical precision he places his hooves. Impeccable balance and surefooted confidence allow him to approach the awaiting band of four subordinate rams below. They rise in salutation as he approaches. The rams have been anticipating his return from the rocky heavens, and now they will precede him down into the moist green valley far below.

The hunter's crude camp is located at the foot of the valley, near where the stream that courses the valley's center begins its steep plunge through thick alders, then willow, and finally spruce. Originating at a glacier near the head of the valley, the stream offers the most pure, chilled water that a man can drink. It has been purified a thousand times by the miles of gravel and pulverized rock that it filters through. To again filter this water would be akin to contaminating it, so he scoops large gulps of it right into his lightweight metal drinking cup, and marvels at its wholesomeness.

He is flanked by the spires of sharp peaked mountains, forming ridges on both sides of this once glacier filled expanse. Blanketed by the cloud that now rests, awaiting the sun to usher it on its way, he has the feeling of being in a large cathedral, with stone pews that run for miles toward a glacial altar.

No time for a hot breakfast today, this hunter has a

rendezvous with destiny.   After pulling on his damp, sweat-stained clothing, he readies a daypack with the tools of a solo rifleman before moving off into the mist to meet a seemingly predictable band of sheep at the edge of a steep grassy meadow.

The rising morning air currents bring the sweet, moist smell of grass and lichen to the old ram. The scent grows stronger as the clouds are cut by the morning sun, its rays warm the grass-covered slopes and moss-covered rocks.   With the air current comes an odd, unfamiliar scent, musty, yet un-alarming – neither the smell of wolf nor bear, therefore unthreatening.

The band of five rams, two of which are in their adolescent years, move across the shale scree just under the heights of jagged rock. The loose, flat rocks provide the least assured footing as they slide and shift beneath perfectly adapted hooves.   The large ram follows behind, trusting the instincts of the younger, more agile rams as rocks tumble to the grassy slopes below. Stopping to observe the other rams as they proceed, he studies them for hesitation or a hint of alarm as they make their way ahead of him.   His eyes scan the valley walls and floor, seeking the origin of the strange scent that occasionally passes his nostrils.   The powerful eyes of the ram can identify danger at great distance, yet he sees nothing but the familiar glacial moraine that he calls his summer home.

The leading ram, the youngest in this band of bachelors - horns curling only slightly as they rise above his head - begins to feed on the tender grass upon reaching it. This grassy slope rings much of the valley, interrupted intermittently by a jagged ridge or an arm of granite boulders that reach toward the peaks.

The morning sun's warmth has caused the cloud to lift, its rays now penetrate to the valley floor. The old hunter treads gently uphill on the right side of the glacial moraine, toward a finger of boulders and shale scree. The boulders will be used as cover during his climb.

A disturbed marmot, which resembles a large squirrel, hops up onto a rock and emits a loud whistle as he approaches, sounding an alarm to all that will listen. He ignores the agitated critter, although annoyed by its having revealed his presence, and continues to climb carefully over large rocks that lead to the point of ambush he had chosen the day before. The rocks appear precisely placed by a talented hand, just like the oranges or apples in a grocery display – if the shopper pulls the bottom one, they all come tumbling into the aisle.

A gentle wind from far up the valley brings the smell of a late summer shower. A large raven circles above.

The rams fan out to feed in earnest upon reaching the steep meadow. They face in all directions, perpetually alert to any danger, and often raise their heads in turn to inspect their surroundings. The moist mouthfuls of grass, with minerals provided by the gravely soil beneath, provide necessary nourishment to the most regal of mountain inhabitants. Getting the nourishment he requires is now a concerted effort, as the old ram has lost a number of teeth in the last year.

A marmot barks a squeaking alarm as it rushes from boulder to boulder farther down the valley. Two of the rams raise their heads to see what the fuss is about, but marmots are known for their unnecessary chatter, so it goes largely ignored.

A cloudbank now hides the sun and a chilly breeze sweeps down from the glacier at the head of the valley home. The current of air has carried away the odd, musty smell, replacing it with the familiar scent of an approaching late-summer shower.

They will feed toward the lower end of the valley before bedding down to digest the morning's sustenance. It is not very far, and the band has done this each day of the preceding two weeks. This has proven to be a very safe route.

The hunter has almost reached the rocky ambush point, and he is now sweating heavily from the strenuous climb. His leg muscles and joints, conditioned by years of mountainous pursuit, are now strained; they are not as flexible or forgiving of his demands as they were in years prior.

One more shale slide to cross before he will reach the rocky outcropping, but the chosen path is much steeper than he had perceived. His instincts tell him to be patient - *find a safer approach* - but he has glimpsed his prize. The band of rams is approaching from farther up the valley, feeding toward his position, so he forges on.

As the sheep graze lazily down the valley, a less mature ram raises its head and approaches the mighty ram. In what appears to be a gesture of respect, yet hinting of a challenge, the subordinate ram moves his head from side to side, then lowers his horns to touch the ground beneath the chin of the lead ram, rolling his nose underneath his own chest to display the back of his head. The dominant one takes a step backward and responds in kind as the subordinate ram lifts his head.

You're not ready to lead this band yet, big boy. The mighty ram thinks. *But it won't be long...*

The subordinate ram moves away after bellowing a snort. He joins the lesser rams and continues to feed down the valley.

The crossing of the last steep shale slide is done on all fours; terrifying even to this seasoned hunter. Just below the shale scree field is a drop that he cannot see over into. The rocks tumble from beneath his feet with each measured step, but it is too late to turn back now, just fifteen or twenty feet higher and he will be at his shooting destination.

Upon reaching his chosen rendezvous at the rocky outcrop, he finds himself hanging on with one hand to maintain his balance. He sees that the rams have stopped, and one subordinate ram seems to be measuring himself against the largest of the rams, whose heavy horns sweep deep before jutting outward on each side. The hunter recognizes this sheep as truly "a trophy to die for".

With his only free hand he awkwardly prepares his rifle to fire by chambering a round and removing his scope cover. The scope cover falls away from him and tumbles below, but without much sound. A light rain begins to fall as the raven, which was circling, is now perched on a far rock. The sheep are between the hunter and the lone raven. *Maybe what they say is true*, he thinks, *that ravens can sense when death is forthcoming, so they wait nearby for their share of the scraps.* Not many of the new hunters have learned the age-old practice of following the lead of the raven to their quarry.

The sky is slowly darkening as the morning progresses, and a light drizzle rolls in from the far end of the valley. *Amusing how quickly the weather changes in these mountain ranges.* The gentle breeze has stopped and once again the acrid, musty smell alerts the larger ram. He raises his head and begins a detailed search for danger along the sides of the grassy meadow.

A short distance away and up the valley, a raven comes to a landing on a large boulder above the band of sheep. The raven stares intently in the direction of the sheep as if waiting for something to happen. One of the subordinate rams has turned, and is high-stepping back uphill, deliberately driving its hooves into the grass at each step. *That's not good.*

The sheep will vanish like dissipating smoke once they feel threatened, the hunter thinks to himself. His heart begins to beat quicker now.

With his rifle lying across a rock, the old hunter rushes to find the larger ram in his scope. The band is only about a hundred yards away, but he must hurry the shot. The safety is instinctively pushed forward. This would be a cinch if his muscles were not straining from holding the awkward position on the steep rock face. He has the large ram quartered momentarily in the scope; it is looking right through him. The ram turns uphill to escape. The hunter fires. The recoil has jarred the rifle out of his shoulder but the hunter sees the huge ram collapse... just as the rock beneath his left foot gives way.

The old ram turns uphill, toward the not-so-distant safety of the lofty perch; then his right eye glimpses a flash. A sound resembling that of thunder booms in the valley and a burning sensation penetrates the chest of the great ram; his muscular back legs fail to respond to his strong desire to flee. The ram's rump collapses beneath him and the subordinate rams trot past, leaving the great ram to his fate.

A prickly numbness overcomes the ram as he falls over onto his right side. With his right eye, he can see nothing but green, the grass that has been his nourishment. His left eye glimpses the second ram, now far away, as it turns – puzzled – to pay homage to the fallen, mighty patriarch. Then all is black.

The patient raven is squawking now...

And the old ram's spirit drifts toward the safety of his lofty perch overlooking its glacial valley home.

* * *

The old hunter scrambles for purchase, but has begun to slide. He is on his belly, sliding through the shale, grabbing with both hands for anything anchored. The rifle that has been with him on countless hunts, in all the ranges of this great land, follows him. He closes his eyes just as the mountain disappears from under him – he is falling now.

The hunter is surrounded by nothing but black emptiness, and can faintly hear the sound of the lone raven as it squawks in the distance.

A piercingly bright light appears, and the hunter feels a stinging numbness flow through his body.

He is now weightless; his spirit floating toward *his* heavenly perch high above the valley.

-- As hunters, we must never forget that in the fulfillment of our passionate yearning, we take the lives of living, feeling, thinking beings; and that our lives also are as fragile as the ones we so willingly take. – Marc

The Billy Goats' Bluff

The rise and fall of the fifteen-and-a-half foot Zodiac inflatable boat, on the swells of the incoming tide, is calming to the recently-launched boater. He is approaching the waters of the mouth of Resurrection Bay, and soon he will be a small being, operating a small craft, in the open water of a very large ocean.

The Gulf of Alaska is an unforgiving place to navigate such a small craft, but the seasoned coxswain is undaunted. He is driven by a desire to access the inaccessible, where the ocean meets the jagged shore of the Resurrection Peninsula to the North and East of the mouth of the bay. For there, dwelling amid the mountains that rise from the water, are the legendary mountain goats of "Billy Goats' Bluff".

There is no wind present on this morning, which accounts for the lack of whitecaps on incoming swells at the cape of the peninsula. That could change very suddenly though, causing what is already considered a dangerous undertaking to become a near-suicidal one. The sky is dark with overcast clouds, but the hunter plows on. With a constant whine of the thirty-five horsepower Mercury outboard engine and the ever-present splashing of water against air-taut gunnels as companions, the alert boater keeps watch ahead for floating debris. Although seemingly vast expanses of nothing but water stretch to and beyond the horizon, a collision with an errant drifting piece of timber or other matter could be catastrophic. To find yourself suddenly treading water – forty-degree water – during late September off the coast of Alaska, is akin to finding yourself suddenly sucked, at twenty thousand feet, from the airliner that carries you. The end result will be the same, except you'll go much quicker in the falling scenario.

He was now making his way toward his landing point.

A meticulous map study followed an earlier flight out to reconnoiter the mountain that the goats call home. The flight, in a *Cessna 206 Sky Wagon*, assured the location of the object of his pursuit, and the study of maps confirmed the presence of a somewhat accessible drainage that empties glacier runoff and rainwater into a swampy cove, just inland from the rocky beach.

If it could be called a beach at all, that is. This particular landing site was more like a boulder field reaching into the water. Sometimes gentle waves lick the rocks; but more often, angry waves and spray pound the shore, slowly eroding the rocks and replacing them with rocks and sand churned up from the ocean's floor. Change is constant where earth meets ocean, a very rhythmic change that relents to the persistent seven-stage onslaught of waves and the rising and falling tide.

As the boater/hunter rounds the cape of Resurrection Peninsula, far from the safety of the boat launch in Seward, he finds himself being lulled into a daydream. He sees the mountain goats below him through the window of the plane as the seasoned pilot executes a cross-control maneuver – a very dangerous thing to do in a place like this, or anyplace for that matter – but he has a perfect view of the goats from his right seat. The animals are seemingly thrown against the steep rock outcropping that rims the horseshoe-shaped bowl below, thrown without certain care in a smattering, like stucco flung at a gray wall. The goats were laying about here and there, without any way up or down.

But we both know that's not true. Mountain goats are the supreme masters of rock footing; able to reach places on steep rock faces that would cause even the best of human climbers to cringe. Although not masters of disguise, with thick white coats of coarse fur, they live their lives virtually unmolested by seeking cover in the crags and cliffs that are unreachable by all but winged beings.

He would have to ambush the goats as they climbed to or from the cliffs, and was willing to wait patiently to make that happen. Patience is likely the more important of the virtues bestowed upon the more successful of hunters.

WHOOSH!

A giant vertical cloud burst from the ocean just forward and left of the bow of the boat, its vapors and spray cascading over the boater. He cuts the throttle and comes to an abrupt stop in the ocean, his overtaking wake pushing the stern of the boat high in the water as it catches up to him.

A large gray dorsal ridge churns the water before him. It emerges just twenty feet in front of the craft, then disappears, followed by a huge fluke more than eight feet across, dripping water as it hangs for an endless moment before slipping silently beneath the surface. He has just happened upon one of the seasonal inhabitants of the ocean waters of Alaska – a gray whale.

Imagine the chances of that.

Imagine the magical beauty of that.

Imagine what would have become of him if the whale, which wants no brush with man, had accidentally emerged from the depths in the direct path of him at that moment.

As it works out, the boater is fortunate only to have made visual contact with one of the planet's largest yet least viewed creatures. Very few humans will have such an opportunity, and even fewer can say that his life was nearly ended by the random surfacing of a gray whale.

Reaching forward, the large male mountain goat raises his haunch into the air, stretching strong, old and sinewy muscles. He is now rested after a full night's respite. In his twelfth year, he has reached full and productive maturity. The billy is draped with long, lush, dingy white hair, dense and evenly distributed over his paunch, torso and chest. Stout legs are generously insulated, giving the appearance of large, baggy, yellow-white pants. His eyes are beady and dark, peering from a pure white mane that tapers to a full-grown beard hanging from under his lower jaw. Ebony-black horns rise from between his ears and curve smoothly up and back toward the sky. They are thick at the bases, tapering evenly to pointed tips.

He steps forward, then leaps near vertically, six feet, to a ledge of rock hanging above his bedding area. From there, the goat climbs sure-footedly over sharp shards of rock to another ledge, which he clears, landing on all fours now twenty feet above the bluff overlooking the ocean and the boulder-strewn valley below. From here, it is a short walk through tangle and alder growth to the grass and lichen covered slopes of the bowl in the mountain that he and nearly thirty other mountain goats call home.

The old goat pauses to urinate, then wallows in his puddle to capture the fresh, pungent scent. *That will assure that my presence is known,* he thinks, as the scent drifts across the bowl to the others of his kind. He is the dominant male goat of the mountain, not that he really has to assert himself, and maybe his musky scent assures that. He ambles over to a group of three mature billies, and they turn and walk down into the valley, toward tender green grass and moss.

It's going to be another beautiful day on the mountain, and a drizzle falls over the valley of the goats as they begin to feed.

The intended landing area is in sight – as verified by the direction arrow on the global positioning system. He had marked the boulder beach utilizing coordinates determined from his map study of the area, and is closing in on relatively calm seas. On very few occasions have hunts worked out exactly as planned, but this is turning out to be one such hunt.

Of course, his good fortune began with the winning of the Resurrection Peninsula Goat Permit, as the securing of a lottery permit in the State of Alaska rests solely in the hands of the hunting gods themselves. Only forty or so permits are allotted for this particular area, and he knows his chances of being drawn are miniscule.

Most hunters in possession of this permit would choose to hunt the peninsula in a more conventional manner, maybe by accessing the mountains by foot to the east of Seward, Alaska, or by arranging a water taxi to one of the many coves that offer protection from the turbulent waters of the bay. But with certain knowledge and experience there is confidence, and the combination of the three can lead a man to do what can be considered foolhardy to some.

The hunter is a local – that is, a resident of Seward, which is a relatively small town situated in a postcard, at the northern end of Resurrection Bay. Mountains rise within the city limits, towering as sky-scrapers tower in some more populated cities. It is a fishing and tourist community, being visited by the large cruise ships during the summer months, and becoming near dormant during the winter. Every photograph taken in this town is cherished by the taker, as there are very few communities to be found in locales as beautiful.

He feels fortunate to be afforded an opportunity to reside in such a lovely place – as anyone should. A commercial fisherman by trade, the boater is very familiar with water, and is comfortable with embarking on a solo trip out of the bay. However, he retains the utmost respect for the inherent dangers that traveling over open water may invite. One must be intimate with his personal limitations and the limitations that nature may bestow – never exceeding them – or dire consequences may result.

Alaska is not only a geographical place; Alaska is an entity, a being of itself, one that allows you to take in its beauty as long as you are reverent of its might. In 'The Great State," you may be afforded only one mistake.

The boat is run aground in choppy seas, and at the last moment, the motor is pivoted to a horizontal position in its transom, allowing the forward momentum of the vessel to carry it onto shore. The boater steps over the carefully stowed gear tied to the aluminum flooring of the boat and plants his booted foot on the rocky shore. A nylon rope, secured to the bow, is utilized to haul the boat aground. He then begins to unload the gear in its entirety, including the very heavy motor and fuel. All must be stowed inland, well above high tide line, in the event of a storm or an unusually high tide.

All's well that begins well, right? And this boater, turned hunter, has planned and rehearsed each detail of the beaching. If the vessel were to be blown away, or carried out by the tide, then what starts as a hunt will quickly become a survival exercise, and there's no sense in that happening as long as it can be prevented.

The hunter has executed his plan perfectly, and now readies his gear for travel up the watershed that stands before him. His backpack and frame contain the necessities to sustain him for up to ten days in the wilderness alone – keeping him relatively warm, fed, and dry. He is armed with a bolt-action thirty-caliber rifle and factory ammunition. There's much fuss about the reloading of ammunition to serve each need, but dead is dead in his eyes. Who's to know whether the projectile hit the animal at twenty-eight hundred feet per second, or twenty-eight fifty, and who cares? His shot should be less than three hundred yards in any event, and the bullet combination chosen for the job is of the heavy-duty variety. If he gets a decent opportunity to take a mountain goat, chances are great the job will get done.

He strikes out to the west and upward, immediately trudging over boulders and large rocks, keeping balance with a third point of contact. The telescoping lightweight trekking pole, which accompanies the hunter on many of his outings, has prevented countless mishaps and provides an extra measure of balance and confidence. In no time he reaches the stream that will take him to the bowl containing the goats. It will be only a short walk where distance is concerned, at just over two miles, but he will quickly gain altitude and sustain a steady climb for the better part of the next seven hours.

There's something about wet feet during a hunt that bothers most people. Hunters will go to great length to keep dry feet, but the end result is usually the same. Feet will become wet eventually during a hunt such as this, so the hunter starts the hike out right by stepping squarely into the first pool of water, soaking the mid-height hiking shoes immediately. He has chosen a lightweight mesh variety that is not waterproof, so that water will be expelled rapidly once taken on. Too much thought put into keeping shoes or boots dry can cause a twisted ankle or a nasty fall from a slippery rock while wearing a heavy pack. That's not to say that he won't pamper his wet feet when he reaches his destination, but for now, he drives on, with little thought put to the cold water that runs around his ankles.

The steep, narrow stream is surrounded by thick growth of alders and the dreaded "devil's club," which closes in behind the hunter. After only a short distance, he can no longer see the rocky shore behind him as he climbs. The alders are thick, their limbs interlocking from both sides, causing him to often climb through, over, and under their boughs. The steep sides of the mountain, just yards to either side, are dense with the spiny nuisance of devil's club, which offers no handhold when encountered. It has large leaves that grow in a canopy from the top of its thick stalk, which is covered with spines that feel like shards of glass when they penetrate unprotected hands or forearms. The hunter wears a pair of heavy work gloves for this reason, but that does not deter the needles from attaching to arms, legs, or anything they contact. The plants grow from a heavy root, parallel to the ground and then jut skyward, causing a springing "club" to smack even the most careful. The devil's doings – for sure.

He makes great time, and pauses often to drink from the stream and readjust gear that has been grabbed and tugged at by the alders. A map study shows that he is nearing an imaginary half-way point and has climbed nearly thirteen hundred feet since stowing the boat. It is early evening, and there is five hours of daylight remaining before he will be forced to make camp. He begins to daydream again about the object of his desire, as he rests in the damp grass that has replaced the alders.

* * *

Three healthy male goats rest in the overcast evening sunlight, having grazed on grass and lichen for most of the day. They are near a large snow pack that is left from the previous winter. It gets smaller by the day, but will hardly melt completely before the snow begins to fall again in the late fall. The melting water is taken into the acres of rocks that it covers, and emerges farther down the mountain in the form of a run-off stream that flows to the sea.

The band of goats has occupied this bowl that separates two mountain peaks for more than two months, and soon it will be time to move to higher ground, toward the wind-swept rocks that will be their winter home. But for now, this is paradise and the smallest of the three rises and bows deep in a stretch before studying the bowl in detail for dark movement. The nannies and kids are at the rim on the far side, as it is customary for them to be apart from the billies for most of the summer.

He searches for danger, usually in the form of a black bear, which sometimes manages to outmaneuver and corner a kid, causing the smell of death to swirl with the wind currents in the bowl. Death comes quickly to the young goat, but not before it bays a terrified warning to the others once caught in the jaws of the bear. Given time, they learn to climb when danger approaches, as even the young can quickly escape to the rocks if given sufficient warning.

The crisp nights of the fall bring heavy coats to all who wear white, and the three billies each look nearly twice their actual size. The older one is such by three years, and is easily distinguished by his dingy coat. His head is large, short, and blocky; adorned with a crown of ebony horns reaching nearly a foot above his head. He is the unofficial keeper of time, and signals the move to and from the bluff that overlooks the ocean.

He rises, stretches boldly, and moves in that direction – it must be time, so the billies amble toward their respective beds over the lip of the bowl. Another lazy day in the bowl comes to an uneventful end.

The hunter has been above the thick vegetation for nearly an hour, making his way now over dry, crushed rock and grass on a rather steep slope. The stream has become a slight trickle, his having climbed above the underground springs that fed it, and he has nearly walked his feet dry. He is moving ever closer to the mountain bowl known to contain the goats, but he has yet to see them and still must traverse farther to the west, gaining five hundred more feet before reaching his destination. The GPS gives the distance as five-tenths of a mile. He wishes that meant something good, but distance can be very deceiving when it is measured on a horizontal plane in such a vertical place. He plods on, now becoming somewhat fatigued by the fifty-five pounds of gear that tugs at his shoulder, and the now heavy rifle that tires his arms.

A chill has permeated the evening air, finding the hunter resting just out of eyesight of the bowl that is his destination. He has glimpsed white spots in the rocks on the far, top rim of the bowl, which is barely visible. A tripod is set up, and topped with his spotting scope. The shapes are studied carefully, revealing a band of nannies with kids. Although he flew the area a week prior, there is always the doubt that floats in the back of the hunter's mind that questions the presence of the quarry in the hunting area. That doubt has just been erased, although no adult male goats are spotted. The hunter searches for a level place for his tent, then begins its set-up with the placing of a ground tarp.

He is comfortably inside his shelter, with gear properly stowed, when the drizzle begins to fall. The cool evening air has brought with it the moisture that is no stranger to these mountains at the close of summer. Water is boiled for a well-deserved dinner, as tired muscles must be fed and hydrated to maintain. This is a very comfortable spot – just out of the immediate range of the mountain goats, and the hunter gives thanks for his safe delivery to their domain.

The temperature will drop into the low forties overnight, and the immediate warmth of his sleeping bag feels like heaven on earth. The drizzle continues throughout the night, providing an audible pattering on the shelter, ushering the hunter to a deep sleep.

Just how much can one experience in a single day? He thinks...

For the right type person, there is a strong comfort in the solitude that engulfs a solo hunter once he is finally alone, surrounded only by the habitat of his prey. It is a feeling of satisfaction and soul-deep peacefulness that pervades only once the distraction of human existence is removed. There seems to be no sense of time, no looming deadline or chore that must be accomplished. The hunt offers an escape to a place where there is no other presence but the spirits of the hunters and hunted that have walked shared ground for the centuries and millenniums preceding.

If you close your eyes you can become that hunter, feeling the same current of air that brushes your cheek, or scent of salt mixed with rock, grass, moss, impending rain, and the smell of your sweat. Relax, and you can imagine that the clothes that drape your body are the robes of slain prey, the shoes that protect the soles of your feet were fashioned from the sturdy skins of the caribou or walrus. You can allow your soul to mingle and consort with the souls that have shared your efforts. Did their muscles strain and hurt on such a climb, as mine do now? Did they feel the necessity to feed tired and sore bodies as easily as I have just done? It is certain that they did, or you would not be in this moment. He passes into the dream world...

In the dream, everything is very dark. *He is floating in what seems to be an icy, wet abyss, but has a very strange sensation of moving forward. There are audible squeaks and groans that echo from the depths below from an undisclosed source, and a very rhythmic splashing off to the right. It is growing louder. A strange pressure surrounds his body, but is becoming lighter with each passing moment. He is moving with a purpose, traveling in the abyss toward a predetermined destination, but it is escaping as he closes the distance.*

A burning fire is growing within his chest and a tingling feeling is creeping toward his extremities. The black turns to dark gray, and now there is a distinguishable difference between the area above and the depths below. The rhythmic splashing is becoming louder, and is approaching rapidly. The urge is to return to the blackness, away from the light, but the tingling sensation grows, and the light becomes a comfort. With a powerful kick of his legs he reaches for it as his lungs feel about to implode. The surface is broken, and he releases the burning sensation in his chest with a powerful exhale, replacing it with a fresh drink of air. But the source of the splashing is dangerously close. With his right eye barely below the surface, he sees a figure sitting upright in the strange craft that is the object of his interest.

The figure is draped in light colors, with a deeply tanned face. In one bony hand, held high above its head the figure grasps something long and pointed, and with a sudden motion, flings the pointed object in the direction of the whale's back. There is an icy sensation in his side, and he pushes for the depths below as a loud scream of elation is heard coming from the strange craft.

It is harder to breathe in the depths, and he reluctantly returns to the light. All is quiet now, but the dark shape hovers above, poised for another strike.

The hunter startles awake and struggles to breathe. He has rolled in his sleeping bag and has become disoriented – unable to find the opening that is his source of fresh air. He panics, searching with his hands, and quickly pulls it over his face, taking large gulps of fresh air.

The lighted dial on his watch reveals that it is after four in the morning. Daylight will return in short order, but now it is black as pitch. The drizzle has subsided, so the hunter lights a candle and lingers in the comfort of his warm chamber while the tiny flame removes the morning chill from the air within the tent.

* * *

On the rocks of the bluff, the three large billies are greeted by a dark purple horizon. Clear, sunny days are a rarity in September in the Gulf of Alaska, but the exceptions to the rule are truly grand. Today will be one of those exceptions.

The drizzle that persisted through most of the night has left the goats of the bowl wet, but the promise of a sunny day will change that. An ocean breeze begins to blow, and the scent of salt from the nearby Gulf of Alaska is present in the air.

The goats rise, only after the sun is well above the horizon, to begin their short but steep ascent up the rock face. In turn, they arrive at the rim of the bowl, the youngest of the three leading the way. Following a short pause to scan the surroundings for danger, they begin to feed toward the east, facing the rapidly rising sun. The nannies are already scattered throughout the bowl, with their kids darting here and there with the playful energy of youth.

Life is grand in the bowl that supports the survival of the mountain goats near "Billy Goats' Bluff."

The hunter has assembled a light pack and frame that will accompany him on the relatively short climb to the bowl containing the goats. It is a welcomed comfort to the tired shoulders that bore the weight of the heavy pack for most of the previous day. His leg muscles pump with newfound fervor at the light load, and he is off with minimal gear toward a bright, sunlit bowl, recessed into the mountains above him.

He walks upward and to the west at a cautious pace for most of an hour before reaching the rock-strewn edge of the bowl. His upward gait has become a crouch, in anticipation of spotting feeding mountain goats just over the rise to his front. He kneels to gather his senses, transforming himself from a hiker to a hunter – the moment of truth may come at any time now, so he eases the bolt of the rifle back to reveal the shells that have been stored in the magazine. In its forward movement, the face of the bolt push-feeds a fat cartridge from the magazine to the throat, and as the bolt lugs seal the round within the chamber, an audible metallic locking sound assures the hunter that the round is properly seated. The safety mechanism is engaged, and the hunt is on.

The rocks are grating against his chest and belly as he crawls forward to a large promontory that will be his vantage point. No goats are visible on the rim of the bowl, which leads him to believe that they may be feeding just ahead of him. And he is right.

The large billy lies resting, rehashing the morning's bounty of late summer grass. The other adult billies lie nearby, and the larger is distinguishable by his dirty coat of what should be pure white. The morning air is brisk, but holds the promise of remaining clear. Such is the rather sedentary life within the safety of the bowl on such a beautiful sunny day.

The ground slopes gently away to the north, with the ridge of the bowl behind them at a distance that will make for a safe getaway should that be necessary.

He begins to doze in the lazy, warm heat of the fall sunlight.

The hunter is prone, scanning the width of the bowl with binoculars.   There are goats virtually everywhere, feeding, grazing, and lying about. Four goats, much larger than the rest, are in beds to his left and above, at a distance that would be safe to judge as five hundred yards or so. There is a large, rather dirty billy among them, and the seasoned goat hunter identifies this goat as worthy of a closer look. He pulls the pack up alongside him and removes a spotting scope. The pack is pushed ahead of him, and the spotting scope rests easily across the top. The focus is crisp and sharp, revealing the large billy to be what he truly is, the patriarch of the entire bowl. The Granddad of all goats, with jet-black, glistening horns rising high above his blocky head. The magnification is increased, revealing to the hunter that the goat is sleeping in the sun, and will probably not be moving, unless disturbed, in the next hour or so at the least.

This will be his goat.

He stores the optics in the pack and leaves it in place. Only the rifle will accompany him in his quest to get closer to the sleeping billy, as excess gear can only draw unwanted attention and inhibit the agonizingly slow stalk that will be necessary from here on.

Pulling the GPS from his pocket, he marks his position, then projects another waypoint five hundred yards to his southwest. That will give him a rough estimate of where the goats are, even when they are not visible. The direction-finding device is left on during the stalk, constantly reminding him of the distance to the target. Of course, this is not the first time he has executed such an operation, as the method has assisted him on many stalks of bedded moose and brown bears in thick cover.

There is a slight depression in the mountain below and left, so he eases back and into it. He is able to follow it upward, sweeping to the east of the goats. He walks at a steep crouch, nearly duck-walking to stay out of the line of sight of the goats. There are others in the bowl, but not within sight.

After two grueling hours of crawling, creeping, hunching, peeking, and creeping again, his GPS reads two hundred thirteen yards. There is a slight rock formation before him that masks his movements from the inhabitants of the bowl, and he is near its lip on the south side. Progressing any further would be too risky, as he is very near the edge of the bowl that drops sharply toward the ocean. He estimates that he is level with the goats or maybe a bit above them, if they have remained in their beds.

With agonizingly slow movements he crawls toward the rock formation, and places himself to the right side of it in order to get a look at the goats. An inch at a time, he proceeds. He must see the goats before they see him, or they will disappear over and into their safe haven on the face of the cliff, which he estimates is now to the left of him at a distance of maybe three hundred yards.

He is lying flat on his stomach with his head cocked to the right. Utilizing mainly his right eye, he inches forward until he can finally glimpse the area where the goats should be lying. *Nothing. There's nothing there.* He pulls the GPS from his pocket, and places it inches before his face. The direction arrow points directly away, toward the now empty rocky beds where the animals were last seen. *Nothing. They're gone.*

The hunter lifts his head to get a view of the entire bowl below, and can immediately see the goats on the far side of the bowl. They appear to be half feeding, and half bedded. That's a good sign – they've not been alerted to his presence – or at least the goats on the other side of the bowl have not been alerted. Forward a little more, and... There they are! Three large billies below at a distance of maybe one hundred and fifty yards, and unaware that they are being watched – stalked – from above. The sun is directly behind him, and his position is near perfect. He is located at the top of the billy goats' bluff.

The youngest of the four goats rises and stretches the muscles of his bulky body in true mountain goat fashion. The others continue to rest, but they are aware that soon they also must rise from lazy beds to feed the strong bodies. At this time of the year, they are grazing *machines*. They must bulk up for the lean winter months when green grass will be but a memory. The goats will cling to the wind-swept cliffs, expending very little energy in order to slowly deplete the fat reserves acquired in the summer and fall months.

They rise in turn, from the youngest to the oldest, which rolls and wallows in his bed before standing. He faces the mid-afternoon sun, which is rapidly moving toward the southern sky. It's the Autumnal equinox, and the sun looms in an path directly over the equator in its receding arc toward winter. For now, its rays are splendid. There are very few days of continuous sunshine in this harsh part of the world.

He follows as the band of billies begins to feed again. Beady, dark eyes scan the cliffs above and the valley below for danger.

The hunter readies his rifle. The bolt remains locked, and the safety is still engaged. He slides the rifle forward slowly, and angles the barrel down toward where the billies should be. Slowly, he inches forward, exposing himself to all before him. The goats are oblivious to his presence as they stand before him at a distance very near the distance he utilized to zero his rifle.

The hunter is now a shooter, and the terminus of the journey is near. It is merely a matter of proper shot placement as the rifle butt is drawn to the pocket of his shoulder. This is the moment of truth, when many hunters fail, for a hunter's pulse quickens when the game animal is sighted; a shooter's pulse deadens, becoming willed, as the nervous energy is redirected – re-channeled into calm confidence.

His cheek is now contacting the stock of the rifle. A trained eye comes immediately to line-of-sight. The post, sitting atop the end of his barrel is seen clearly through the ghost-ring aperture of the Lyman peep sight. The post is centered squarely on the shoulder of the large, dingy mountain goat. With both eyes open, the shooter sees that the goats are widely dispersed. If his bullet exits, it will pass harmlessly down the mountain. The goat in his sights looks directly at him, toward the sun.

The hunter's left eye closes, instinctively, to pass the deadly duty to the shooting eye. A deep breath is taken as the safety is pushed forward with a thumb. There's an audible click. He exhales half and pauses. The post is crisp, and just behind the goat's right leg – one last blink of the shooting eye as he increases tension on the tip of his trigger finger.

The great goat finds himself again glancing toward the sun. Its warmth is strangely attractive to him on this day, as it now hangs just above the rim of the bowl. A small yearling goat bays from a distance, and a slight breeze brings the smell of grass being pulled from the ground by the other billies...

The breath of air that carried the sweet scent is blown from his lungs as the one hundred eighty grain bullet passes cleanly through them. In one millionth of a second, tremendous pressure creates a huge cavity in the animal's chest, then his heart and lungs violently collide as the vacuumous cavity collapses.

His legs falter, and he is straining to gather another breath, which never really comes. He climbs to his feet and turns toward the safety of the rim of the bowl, walking directly into the sunlight. Blood sprays from his left side with each strained breath.

He is weak, and can no longer stand. The billy's legs will no longer hold him, and he falls forward, facing uphill.

A strange figure rises, blocking the sun which rests on the edge of the bowl from reaching his face, as the great billy strains now just to keep his eyes open. The figure raises odd, spindly limbs above his head and the sun's warmth is replaced by a numbing chill. He lies now in the shadow of his tormentor and quickly drowns in the frothy blood that fills his punctured lungs.

The two male billies momentarily look on in puzzled horror, before fleeing toward the other goats on the far side of the bowl.

The shooter quickly ejects the spent cartridge as the billy collapses. It was a perfect shot – clean through both lungs. The goat regains his feet and turns uphill displaying a tremendous will to live – walking directly toward the hunter, who stands unknowingly at the top of the entrance to the bluff.

He contemplates a follow-up shot, but dismisses the notion, as the goat is far from the rim and fading fast. It falls forward, and the hunter stands, on the rim of the bowl, his arms outstretched above him in a moment of glory.

The hunter senses the sun's warmth on his back as the tingling, chilling sensation of triumph fills his soul.

This is how far one can come in a single day.

-- *If you're thinking that this story ended abruptly, then how do you think the old billy goat feels about his abrupt end? We must relish each breath of air as if it may be our last. – Marc*

When the things we love
Are taken for granted,
Then granted;
The things we love are taken.

-- Marc, Jan. 2004

Broken Instinct

Thinking back, he probably should never have corrected her. Instinct is deeply rooted, and he had no business tampering with it. If only she could understand the weight of this very dire situation; but she's much too obedient now, and just sits there whimpering, seemingly helpless to his plight.

The pale yellow, eighty-five pound Labrador retriever pawed lightly at the snow, fearing the sharp scolding of her master, but it would never come.

An ad in the paper proclaimed, *"Labrador-mixed Puppies - $200. Call early morning or late evening. East Anchorage."* A number was provided which betrayed the owner's real location, which was over an hour drive from the city, so they hesitated at making the call. He and his wife had longed for companionship for some time now, and lived in the perfect home for a puppy; an ample yard with lots of stumps to dig around, and a long driveway in which to call a dog back before it might reach the street.

What could the mix be? They questioned. It would be horrible to have a retriever mixed with something like a Rottweiler, or, God forbid a poodle or some other relatively useless member of the canine family. He wanted a companion, a loyal, obedient friend to accompany him on long hikes, and after some training, a hunting dog that would walk at his side, betraying only those who might cause him harm. In Alaska, danger may come in the form of a bear or maybe a cow moose with a nearby calf, and close interactions with bears or moose in their own comfortable habitat can be a serious breach of good health for the human.

The wife, on the other hand, sought a more personal attendant to keep her company during the outings of her husband, protecting her from harm and providing physical warmth, more of a lap dog perhaps.

She placed the call and they brought home the sole yellow puppy of the litter, which contained mostly black puppies strong in their Labrador characteristics.

Her name would be "Guerra", pronounced as "wedda", which means the little light-skinned girl of the family, in Spanish. Her coat was pale yellow, the color of straw, with thick guard hair famous in water dogs. A strong frame and thick chest tapered to boxy hips and a tail that curved straight up and over her back. This tail betrayed her mixed breeding, which incidentally was of the Husky family, which are the heartiest of the Alaska breeds.

In the two following years after her adoption, Wedda lived up to the sum of the expectations of both, staying just ahead on walks, alerting at the presence of other animals and becoming a great home guardian, never straying far from the yard. She lived for the long walks in the mountains near their home, climbing up and over ridges with the surefootedness of a goat and the tireless endurance of the famed dogs of the "Iditarod." Upon venturing too far ahead, she would turn and sprint back to the leader of the jaunt – tongue dangling and mouth and eyes held in the look that could only represent a smile, as if to say, "Hurry up, there's much more to explore before we return to the car."

A loving pet, well cared for and in good health is an insatiable sponge, and can be made to understand literally thousands of distinct commands. However, there are actions intrinsic, or instinctual to even the most domesticated of man's friends. Instincts can vary widely among canine breeds, but all have evolved from the wolves and wild dogs that must have hunted voraciously and dug in deep to ensure the survival of the pack and to escape the harsh climates in which they thrived. Of course, having become dependent upon humans to provide food and comfort, their keen instincts have been dulled over the thousands of years since the taming of the first wild dog. But you'll find that if your dog misses only a couple of meals due to the laziness or carelessness so characteristic in the human species, it will quickly revert to its wild ways, maybe capturing and devouring your neighbor's cat in order to fill the yearning that dwells deep inside.

Wedda was no exception, and her dominant instincts dwelt just below the surface of her thick blonde hairs. She loved to dig and she did not confine her digging to the stumps in the yard. No, she dug up the newly planted shrubs and trees, freed large rocks from their subterranean prisons, and even attempted to dislodge the garage's concrete foundation from its footing, only stopping when she could shove her head underneath. It was almost an acting-out, because every time she would be left alone at home, attached by a cable run that ran the length of the yard, there would be fresh excavation for the master to find. And he would be furious at its discovery – calling her to the spot, where she would cower to the ground, eyes blinking and snout drooping in a frown. She would get a terrific scolding, and he would force her nose into the ground, screaming "No, Wedda! No Digging! *Nnnooo Diigggiing!"*

Wedda would sulk once he let go, retreating to the far end of the run to escape his displeasure. Remaining there until he called much later for her to return to him, she would do so in a slinking manner, and with the broken spirit of a beaten dog – but without the beating, of course.

She loved her master more than life and longed for his more tender voice, the one that told her that her actions were good. He would lay his hands on her lovingly and things would be better again, but until then she was broken, and her instinct to uproot things and displace earth were broken with it. This was a terrific nut for the master to crack, but eventually she could be trusted not do dig when out of direct site.

Residing in Anchorage is a truly unique experience, as it is very common to be sitting at your table drinking a soothing cup of coffee and enjoying the local newspaper when a moose walks through your yard. It may pause to browse tender twigs from the deciduous trees, or maybe to peel a bit of willow bark if the season happens to be late winter.

Wedda had a strange tolerance for the huge ungulates that visited her yard. She would sit upright attentively, studying the moose's movements, and as it sauntered away she would follow along, careful of the visitor's minimums for approachable distance before becoming defensive, or even deadly. Many a dog has been stomped to death in Alaska for violating the space of the planet's largest member of the deer species. She must have understood that moose browsed the ground under her feet long before yard boundaries were established and foundations were laid. It also helps when you share your living room with the shoulder-mount of a rather large bull. Maybe it was like having a big brother who never really paid much attention to you. He just gazes longingly across the room and out the window from his stud-bolted position on the wall, his bark-peeling days having been brought to an abrupt end by a hunter who desires his sweet, delicious meat and appreciates his grand, palmated antlers.

It was no secret when the master was preparing for an adventure. He would begin by rooting around in the garage, preparing a pack filled with necessary items. Once the collapsible dog bowl was thrown in, that was it – she would be going, and an outing could only be mere hours away. Wedda would quiver with excitement as he pulled his hiking pants and shirt from the closet that contained his special clothes. She paced back and forth near the front door to ensure that no one left her behind. This time however, events were a bit different. It was the dead of winter, and there was a foot of fresh snow in the yard. A strange sled was prepared in the place of a pack, and he would pull it behind him.

They set out by car on a very cold morning, in the general direction of where the usual walks took place, except this time they traveled farther, reaching the parking place after three hours of slow travel through occasionally heavy snowfall. The master secured a pack frame to his back, to which were attached two long poles leading to the sled which was dragged behind. Wedda led for a while, but after an hour she began to tire of breaking trail through the chest-deep snow, so she fell behind into the trail left by the long plastic sled. It cut a large trench nearly a foot deep in the thick, wet powder. The master seemed to be laboring too, but this time not under the weight of a heavy pack, which was how he usually traveled. He stopped occasionally to catch his breath and to adjust the gear in the sled, which was wrapped in a blue tarp to prevent snow from entering. Hefty, taut bungee cords were stretched across the sled and back further securing the load from shifting. During these brief pauses she would guard the trail ahead, the trail that led deeper into the steep, snow-blanketed Kenai Mountains.

The mountains rose nearly straight up on either side of the direction of travel, and after nearly five hours of venturing deeper into the snow-white void, and upon having gained nearly two thousand feet of altitude, they stopped. The master began to arrange for an overnight camp as light was beginning to fade in the valley, yet he was not hurried. A tent was erected in short order, and nearly all gear with the exception of the sled was placed inside. He prepared a meal of dehydrated lasagna for himself and a warm bowl of dried dog food with hot water added for Wedda. That was a very special treat, and it was her first experience with food other than the normal room-temperature variety that she had grown accustomed to eating. Maybe it was her reward for such a hard day's travel and maybe it would be necessary to allow her to sleep warm in the bitter cold, but it was a welcome and gratifying meal, none-the-less.

The night was exceptionally quiet, with just a breeze stirring from the upper end of the valley. A small lantern was lit inside the tent, providing warmth and light for its two occupants. The master prepared a place for her to sleep, just inside the zipper enclosure of the front of the tent, utilizing a half of a sleeping mat of closed cell foam, and then a thicker pad for himself underneath a lofty sleeping bag.

After full-dark they wandered outside for a brief look around, and the sky danced with waves of green transparent clouds in a sea of black. The aurora borealis cast an eerie glow on the snow, causing the master to remark aloud of its splendor. It was very nice to share such a moment with him, and he rubbed her ears and spoke in the kind voice to her before wrapping her in her dog jacket, which was made of the same insulation as his sleeping bag. Before long they retired to the tent and he read while she lay curled up at his feet. She slept undisturbed through the night in the presence of the dancing green light, and the slight sound of a winter breeze as it brushed the tent with a delicate hand.

Morning comes late in the winter months, and the reduced daylight hours require that daytime activities be compressed, maximized, in order to take full advantage of available, yet diminished light. It's almost like twilight even when the sun is at its apex, and in the right, or wrong place, it may never crest the mountains if you happen to be within their shadow.

The occupants of the tent stirred long before daylight, and instant coffee was being prepared by the master in the light of the lantern. Snow was being melted to make the hot water, and some of it was poured over a doggie biscuit for Wedda before coffee was made. This was an extended trip by her standards, but the reason for the trip was yet to be revealed. So often they had marched to a distant alpine lake or ridge, stayed a while, and then turned for the car and home. This time they were remaining outside, and it puzzled her as to the exact goal of their outing.

Most often he had left her behind and come home days later with a strange animal for her to inspect. Some were pure white, with long, tan curled horns. Some had short, black horns, but the same white hair while others were dark brown or black, smelling of evil. She would be frightened by them, and the hair along her back would raise instinctively when in the presence of the large brown ones with the long claws. This time he had taken her on one of his longer trips and she could tell by his movements – the way the clumsiness of his mannerism and movement was replaced with premeditation – that he was hunting, and that they had come for one of the animals that he occasionally introduced her to. She was not sure how she was to help with the hunt, having never been an active participant, but she was confident that he would make clear to her a way of assisting. She would just await his command. But for now, the area near the camp needed exploring, so she made an ever-widening circle around the tent, inspecting and sniffing each branch that protruded from the snow.

What a glorious outing this was going to be, she thought.

The master emerged from the tent and donned heavy wool bibs for protection from the cold. Retrieving a spotting scope and tripod from the gear in the tent, he constructed a viewing platform, with the upside-down sled as a seat and the tripod and scope erected just forward of his feet.

He trained the looking device up the drainage toward the pass at the valley's terminus. Its steep sides appeared as a wall in his view and the pass appeared as a saddle resting between two slight peaks, one on the right and another on the left as he viewed them.

A recent flight in a friend's *Cessna 180* betrayed the winter range of a small band of caribou of the Kenai herd, stationary on the far side of that saddle. His possession of a drawing permit for one caribou assured him of an opportunity to get out for some winter camping, with the added bonus of a chance to take a winter caribou, long in hair, and lean of excess fat because of the limited forage. Caribou must work diligently for very little during the long winter and can hardly afford to move about in their usual meandering way as calories expended would stand very little chance of being replenished during the barren season.

He plotted a route that would take him to the saddle. The caribou should be somewhere in the adjacent drainage on the other side of the pass.

He marked the location of his camp with the GPS that lay at the foot of his sleeping bag, and tucked it away securely in the front pocket of his shirt. The low light was improving, so he gathered all essential gear for shooting, skinning, quartering, bagging and hauling a caribou out of the mountains. He would wear his snowshoes and pack a pair of crampons. A hiking pole was utilized, and an ice-axe was packed in the sled, just in case the terrain turned steep. A lunch of ramen noodles and a power bar, and a full meal for dinner would be packed as well, should the task take longer than necessary. His rifle would be slung over the vertical bar of his pack frame, within easy access and to assure that a shot could be managed in the event the caribou pleasantly surprised him.

Wedda would have to accompany him as she would not stand for being left back alone at camp, and he couldn't just tie her to a protruding willow branch for fear of attack by a passing wolverine, or maybe an errant wolf. The wild ones are capable of such atrocities, especially during winter, and she feared no other creature, in her loving way.

The band of caribou lounged lazily in the morning light. A small herd of thirty-one occupied this valley, as to accumulate in numbers too great assured that enough browse for all would not be found on the snow-covered mountainside. They would soon rise and begin the short climb to the top of the ridge, which had been swept by the broom of the winter wind that blew intermittently down the valley, uncovering the dried grasses and moss on the high slopes and ridges.

The leader of the herd was a very old female. She had parented many in this particular group and some in the distant others who occupied the adjacent drainages within the range. Her matriarchal instincts were relatively keen, as was measured by her ability to guide the band to food and away from the marauding predators which often followed in the white land.

The heavy snows of this particular winter had laid a protective blanket on the slopes below them, allowing only the longer-legged of the valley to access the higher ridges at any pace that would be considered predatory. She would simply disappear over the ridge with the small herd in tow, and the followers would tire long before reaching the top, or would quit upon reaching the crest of the ridge only to see the band escaping around a distant peak, having gained too much ground to justify a pursuit.

With wide, cloven hooves they pawed at the snow beneath, uncovering a here-and-there patch of moss or grass to sustain them for the day, or the hour, depending upon its size and quality. This was life in winter. Rest a lot and eat what little one could find in order to make it to the green pastures of spring.

She urged the band to the top of the ridge for the morning's grazing.

The master and Wedda made their way toward the far end of the valley at a much quicker pace today than on the day before. No doubt this was due to the decreased load in the sled, having made a comfortable camp a mile or so back down the valley. If fortunate, the load would be much greater on the way back.

Glassing the ridges intermittently with binoculars strapped securely across his chest, the hunter/master strained to glimpse movement on the ridge near the pass. It was still early, and the sun's light was dim and not actually rising to crest the tips of the mountains yet. He guessed the temperature to be near ten degrees, and the snow was powdery and fresh having fallen two nights prior during a rather heavy winter storm.

This was a particularly snowy year, as even in Anchorage records indicated that above normal precipitation was being experienced. The mountains always received more as a result of their higher altitude, but his snowshoes were doing a terrific job of keeping him on top of it all and making great time toward the heights. Wedda was now struggling to keep up with the sled, but overall making progress at near the same rate. She proved to be very tireless in her young age and was wearing an obvious smile while bounding through the chest-deep snow.

The matriarch reached a wide plateau on the ridge. Here they would graze for a while, the majority of the powder having been blown away to reveal patchy areas of dried lichen. Meandering about, the band began pawing on the near side. A sloping hill lay farther up the ridge, and beyond it were the mountain peaks.

The master froze in his tracks ahead of her. He was again acting with that predatory peculiarity and now whispering for her to sit. She sat, upon his command, and began to look around to determine the reason for his abrupt stop and change of tone.

High above them were strange animals on the snow. This was the object of the master's behavior, and his slow movements showed that he was watching them in the same way that an intruding dog from down the street was studied during his approach, before revealing his true trespassing intention. It was only then that the warning was delivered.

As the hunter crouched low to the snow, studying the suddenly appearing caribou high above, Wedda was sure that at any moment now her master would bark.

This would be perfect, he thought. Having not traveled very far from camp, it would be relatively simple to remove the carcass from here. They milled on the ridge above, and he would either need to get a bit closer, or the caribou would have to move down the rather steep slope below them in order for this to work out.

Judging the distance roughly by eye, it seemed that the shot would be about four hundred yards. Their location above him at such a sharp angle meant to him that he would not hold over, but steady his sight just above his expected point of impact, but they would need to ascend a bit to give him a backstop of white before a shot would be attempted.

No apparent bulls – or at least no antlers present. This was not much of a trophy hunt anyway, this late in the year. *Just come down the slope a bit, and one of you will be mine,* he thought.

The band fed to the far side of the wind-blown spot, some lingering near center of the ridge. The matriarch approached the distant edge to inspect the valley that lay below. No movement or danger was apparent, so maybe this would be as good a spot as any to spend most of the morning. The sun would soon kiss the slope here, so she would encourage remaining in this area to conserve the recently consumed energy. She approached the edge of the valley below and was swallowed up to her stomach in blown snow. Followed by a half-dozen other caribou of the band, they all sank immediately at the leeward side of the wind-swept clearing.

Her instinct warned her to quickly move them away from the steep, deep snow. This was not a good place...

"HHHHWWWWUUUMMMFFFFF" was the sound as the blown-snow cornice gave way beneath them.

The hunter was crawling back toward the sled when he heard the strange sound from above. The mountain of snow was racing toward him. "Wedda, go!!!", he screamed as he was swept under.

A sensation of falling, swimming in a sea of white was replaced quickly by paralysis. Only a moment later the aerated snow was now locked up like dried cement around him, the pressure of tons of ice coming to an abrupt stop. Nothing more than his head and left shoulder were above the ice, but his left arm was uselessly twisted behind him across his back. He wiggled his toes successfully, but he could not move his fingers.

Immediately, he became very, very cold.

Wedda had managed to free herself from the icy trap. Her lesser weight was her saving grace, as she did not sink as the master did during the sweep. She sat shivering with bone-piercing cold, nervously anticipating her master's emergence from the ice. Reaching forward, she licked his face, worried that he did not seem to be in control of this situation that had befallen them.

Through near-frozen jaws, he whispered, "Wedda, dig."

Thinking back, he probably should never have corrected her. Instinct is deeply rooted, and he had no business tampering with it. If only she could understand the weight of this very dire situation; but she's much too obedient now, and just sits there whimpering, seemingly helpless to his plight.

The pale yellow, eighty-five pound Labrador retriever pawed lightly at the snow, fearing the sharp scolding of her master, but it would never come.

Minutes later, his breathing ceased.

-- Some pre-dated instincts should never be broken. May our ability and desire to hunt be one of those instincts. — Marc

Part II

More On Hunting Gear And Tactics

Caribou/Moose Hunt Packing List

Rifle
- Ammo
- Bore Snake
- Oil
- Scope Cover
- Tape for Bore
- Boresight tool

Food
- Brkfst Mix
- Nuts
- Dried Fruit
- Jerky
- Power Bars
- Noodles
- Meals
- Coffee/Tea
- Gatorade
- Water Bottle
- Hydration bag
- Duct Tape

Archery
- Bow / Case
- Arrows
- Tab / Release
- Quiver

Packing
- Frame
- Knee Braces
- Lashing
- Towel
- Trekking Pole

Regulations
- License
- Tags
- Sheep
- Caribou
- Bowhunter I.D.?
- Bear Tag
- I.D.

Optics
- Bino's
- Spotting Scope
- Tripod

Cooking
- JetBoil
- Fuel
- Xtra Fuel
- Utensils
- Lighter(s)
- Skillet
- Spatula

Sleeping
- Wiggy Bag
- Pad
- Light
- Tent, complete
- Ground Tarp

Clothing
- Hunting pants
- Supplex Bottoms
- S.pplex Top
- Worsterion Top
- Underwear Top
- Underwear Bottoms
- Fleece Top
- Fleece Bottom
- Socks x 4
- Rair Top
- Rain Bottom
- Stocking Cap
- Boots
- Long Underwear Top
- Long Underwear Bot.
- Hat
- Gloves
- Mosquito Headnet
- Barren Ground Jkt.
- Traveling clothes

Safety
- Satellite Phone
- Whistle
- Mirror
- EPIRB
- First Aid Kit

Skinning
- Knife
- Steel
- T.A.G. Bags
- T.T.C.
- Folding Saw
- Citric Acid for meat
- Headlamp

Extras
- Maps
- Plastic Bag
- GPS
- Camera
- Batteries
- Cash
- Checks
- Hip Boots
- Book to read
- Hatchet
- Marking Tape
- Lantern
- Tarp for meat
- Moose Call

Toiletries
- Paper Towels
- Garbage Bags
- Wipes
- Batteries
- Lighter
- Mosquito Juice
- Vitamins
- Ibuprofen
- Sunscreen
- Sunglasses
- Toothbrush/Paste
- Dish soap

Drinking
- Purifier
- Iodine Tabs
- Collapsible container(s)
- Garbage bags
- Funnel
- Chapstick
- Extra Duffel
- 60qt Cooler
- Camp shoes
- Claritin

To the Airport !
- **Rifle Case**
- **Cooler/Duffel**
- **Pack**
- **Carry-on**
- **Tickets/Itinerary**

Building a Complete Gear List

You've just dropped your first payment for the hunt of a lifetime... A self-guided Alaska hunt! In eight short months you and a couple of your closest buddies will be waking up out on the unforgiving tundra of Western Alaska.

"Will I be properly prepared for anything that the Alaska experience will dish out?" should be your first question, as even the most experienced of home-range hunters are rendered unsure of themselves once placed in unfamiliar surroundings. Alaska can be the most enjoyable, beautiful place to the properly prepared, or it can seem ugly and relentlessly unforgiving to the improperly equipped of adventurers.

Your investigation into the climate of the area of your hunt reveals that you could be exposed to temperatures from the low 20's all the way up to the mid 60's. Great! – That temperature range includes frost, snow, sleet, rain, wind and sun. Oh yeah, and bugs. Just about anything that can go wrong has to be prepared for, and additionally, you will be engaged in activities such as hiking, shooting, skinning and quartering, packing, and camping. All this, while attempting to remain reasonably dry and comfortable!

Rest assured that there is no need for actual despair or

sleepless nights while turning the pages of your calendar toward your travel date. But you must immediately begin preparing an appropriate gear list, and in an *organized* manner that will assure that most, if not all, of your needs will be met.

The key word is ORGANIZED. In order to ensure that all activities and weather elements will be covered, we must first arrange our gear list to cover the two most important aspects of the trip: (1) Items important to the hunt and (2) items important to health and comfort.

Under category (1), *Items important to the hunt*, you should then list the following: Regulations/Licenses, Shooting, Glassing, Calling, Packing, and Skinning/Butchering. These are your sub-categories that are geared toward the legal taking and removal of game. Of course, add or subtract categories according to your specific needs.

Grab yourself a blank sheet of paper and simply write one of the sub-categories on it in bold letters, then begin listing items of importance that have to do with that category. For instance: Shooting – Rifle (or Bow), 1. Case – hard and soft, 2. Ammo, 3. Bore Snake, 4. Oil, 5. Scope Cover, 6. Bore-sighting Tool. That short list should cover everything from getting your rifle to the hunting area, to shooting it, and then cleaning it for transport back home.

Another example: Packing – 1. Packing Frame, 2. Knee Braces, 4. Lashing, 4. Trekking Pole. Those items cover every aspect of the packing of your game back to the point where it will be removed from the field.

Now, continue until you have listed all of the activities

important to the hunt. Then, under category (2), which are *items important to health and comfort*, you should list the following: Food, Cooking, Drinking, Sleeping, Clothing, Safety and Toiletries and Extras.

An example under this category would be: Sleeping – (List) 1. Sleeping bag, 2. Sleeping Pad, 3. Small Flashlight, 4. Tent, 5. Ground-Tarp. Or, Drinking – (List) 1. Water Bottles and Bladder, 2. Purifier, 3. Iodine Tablets, 4. Collapsible 3-gal. Container.

The manner of listing that I have demonstrated above will produce a very complete list, being that all activities of the hunt are covered, and then the gear to perform each activity is listed. I have found this to be extremely useful, and although I am an Alaska resident, often venturing into the wilds of the "Last Frontier" on short outings, I never attempt an outing without checking my gear lists to ensure that I have covered all of the possibilities, including; bugs, weather, warmth and food.

Remember, in Alaska, you may only be offered one mistake.

Once you've prepared your personal gear list for your trip and have compared it with the list of your hunting partners, you can now begin to eliminate redundant items that can be shared within your hunting party.

Get shopping!!! The purchases of items that are on your list but you do not own can be spread over a greater period of time by planning early. This may soften the blow – Yes, the blow – that your spouse delivers to you when he/she finds the receipts. You can explain how you are carefully timing your purchases in order to least impact the funds of the family! You'll be applauded for your forethought and obvious attention to the placing the needs of the family first. (I have heard of this happening, but have not actually seen it myself. Please contact me if you have a good experience, I'd like to document it for those of us who usually don't.)

In the preparation of your gear list, it may be necessary to pay particular attention to weight compliances or constraints that may have been placed upon you by the airlines, or maybe an air taxi that will be transporting you to the field. Many of the bulkier items can be rented at your hunting destination, thus limiting your need to move through the "airport experience" with excessive gear. Inquire from your outfitter about these services in order to save from having to purchase or transport the items that can be rented or borrowed. It's referred to as a "drop camp".

Always strive for simplicity in the preparation of your list, and delete the items that do not have legitimate purpose. Once you're all done, make a "short list" of the bulk items that you will take as you leave your home – 1) Gun case, 2) Pack, 3) Duffel, 4) Carry-on,

Now make your gear list more useful and readily adaptable by inputting it on your computer on a spreadsheet program such as Microsoft's *Excel*, and update it as your needs change. My gear-needs change with the weather and it's nice to be able to tweak my various gear lists as my hunts become more sophisticated, or as I replace worn gear with lighter or newer versions. My sheep/goat hunting gear list is much lighter and in many instances less comfortable than my caribou/moose hunting gear list because of the vast differences and challenges that are posed by each hunting situation, therefore I keep more than one complete list. You should also for all your hunts away from home, as an elk hunt in the west will require more forethought than a deer hunt out your back door.

Come prepared for anything that Alaska may be able to dish out, and you will find that you will be rewarded with memories that will last a lifetime. Come unprepared and your memories will be just as lasting, but very unpleasant.

If you need further assistance compiling a gear list that you are comfortable with, refer to Book One, *"Hunting Hard...In Alaska! Prepare Yourself To Hunt 'The Last Frontier'"*, or feel free to contact me directly through www.HuntingHardInAlaska.com. I would be happy to answer any questions you may have in order to better prepare you for you Alaska hunt.

Inflatable - Packing List

Pro Pioneer	Oars	Seats/Straps
Carry Strap	Oar Rights	PFD(s)
Yellow Strap	Oar Sleeves	
	Oar Saddle >	**Oar Saddle**
		Neoprene
Boat Kit		8 straps
Pump	**Paddles**	Wing Nuts
Hose		Oar Locks
Fitting		
Xtra fitting		
Repair Kit >	**Repair Kit**	
Bowline	Glue	Moth Balls
Sternline	Large Patches	
Nylon Straps	Round Patches	
Xtra Pump	Tolulol	**Saddle Bag**
Duct Tape	Abrader/roller	Wiggy Bag
Sponge	Rags	Raingear
Gloves	UV protectant	Water Shoes
Xtra Wing Nuts	Valve Wrench	**Small WP Bag**
Xtra Ring Clips	Screwdriver	**Float Tote**
Bungee Balls	Multi-tool	**Cargo Net**
Aligator Clips	Scissors	
	Thread/Needles	Sunglasses
	Hemastat Pliers	
	Braided Fish Line	Blast Match

Sleeping Warm in the Cold

In our adventures into the wilds of North America, we, as outdoor enthusiasts, are very demanding of our equipment. The finest gear is researched and selected to support us in our efforts, and we spend large sums of money with the assumption that we get what we pay for.

The best that money can buy is useless, however, unless we take personal measures to ensure that our gear performs on a level near our expectations. For instance, the most accurate of rifles is rendered mediocre in the hands of an incompetent marksman, just as the possession of quality optics will not guarantee that animals will fill your field of view each time you set the scope on the tripod. The user must become proficient in the capabilities and limitations of his equipment, and adjust his performance accordingly to stretch the effectiveness of the gear to its maximum efficiency and utility.

Sleeping bags are not an exception to that rule. Upon establishing camp at the end of a hard day's play in the wild, we often expect that by zipping ourselves into the cozy cocoon of the latest of innovative marvels of the sleeping bag industry, we will sleep warm. As is often the case, this misconception leads to restless sleep at best, and much cursing and grumbling about having not brought, or bought, enough bag. The usual result is the outdoorsman owning a sleeping bag for each occasion; one for summer, fall, winter, and one for extremely cold conditions. That can get very expensive, at least, and cause another headache when it comes time to pack for a hunt. Which bag do I take? Is weight a factor or is comfort more important?

Just as we must become proficient marksmen in order to perform to the level of our rifles, it is equally important that we become proficient sleepers in order to sleep comfortably at the stated temperature ratings of our sleeping bags. Your rifle will not shoot the target unless you point it precisely at the target and pull the trigger. In the same manner, a sleeping bag will not warm you unless you first warm the air within the bag. In order to do that, you must attend to the factors contributing to warm sleep, and they are as follows: shelter, air temperature, ground temperature, moisture, body temperature, and fuel for sustained warmth. Each of these factors can be controlled or otherwise prepared for prior to crawling into the bag, thus greatly increasing the opportunity for a restful and warm night's sleep in the cold.

Ambient air pressure is the weight of the column of air that rises above you from the surface of your skin to the atmosphere, and on a clear day, can approach fifteen pounds of pressure per square inch. It is of primary importance that you put something between your sleeping bag and that column of air because its weight will force cold air into your bag. A tent, structure, or lean-to are all excellent barriers, and will greatly diminish the effect of air pressure. That's rule number one: always put something substantial between yourself and the atmosphere to improve your chance for a good night's rest. All this and we haven't even discussed rain!

Air temperature is managed by insulating yourself from the surrounding air. This is done by first selecting an appropriate sleeping bag for the occasion, and the first consideration should be the efficiency of the insulation within a sleeping bag and its potential for loft. Loft creates distance between your warm body and the cold surroundings and slows the movement of the warm air toward the cold. Rule number two: choose a sleeping bag that is appropriately rated near or below the temperature that you will experience.

Cold ground beneath your sleeping bag will immediately drain heat from your body; therefore you must properly insulate yourself from the ground by the use of a sleeping pad(s). The level of insulation required will be dictated by the particular situation, and if it is known that you will be sleeping on frozen ground, you must plan accordingly. As a general rule, the number of pads must double, or thickness of your sleeping pad(s) must double in an extremely cold environment. What was comfortable in the summer may not be sufficient for winter camping so attention must be paid to this detail before expecting too much of too little padding. Should your padding prove insufficient, dry clothing can be spread beneath the sleeper to provide additional comfort.

A raised cot alone will not insulate you from the cold. The cold air circulating beneath the cot will have the same effect as sleeping on bare ground if a sleeping pad is not used.

If caught in a survival situation, without the proper gear for sleeping in the cold, and fire is an option, coals can be buried beneath the sleeper. If the ground is frozen, or fire is not an option, the small bows and branches of trees or bushes will provide some insulation from cold, hard ground. Man-made pads are the rule, and natural insulation is the exception. If you short-change this detail, you in effect short-circuit your ability to sleep warm and comfortable. Therefore, rule number three is: purposely and properly insulate yourself and your bag from the ground.

Rule number four: manage moisture. Let's start from the outside and work our way in. You've already erected a tent to protect you from rain or snow, so you've got that covered if you have a dry sleeping bag and can keep it dry. Select a bag that does not readily hold moisture, as your body heat will work overtime heating the water when trapped within your bag. Additionally, wear only dry, synthetic sleeping clothing, like light or medium-weight long underwear. An extra, complete set of undergarments should stay in your tent and only be worn for the purpose of sleeping warm. If necessary, sacrifice warmth and comfort during the active part of the day in order to sleep warm and dry at night.

Sleeping bags that will allow moisture to pass from your body, through the bag, to dissipate in the cool air above are most efficient, because your body will be warming drier air and insulation, and this will require less effort on the part of your core heater. A synthetic insulation is more effective at allowing moisture to pass through your bag. Down traps moisture over time, especially on extended outings where the temperature stays below freezing.

The sleeping pad you've selected should not trap moisture as it passes from your back to the pad. A pad that is ridged or textured, allowing a flow of air to remove moisture is best and will not create puddles of moisture under your bag and mat. This may ultimately seep into your sleeping bag and steal warmth that would be more efficiently used.

Air flow within your tent or shelter, although cool, is good because it will remove excess moisture. If you seal your tent completely, you will notice much more moisture buildup on the inner surface of your tent. This will ultimately lead to damp, clammy equipment and clothing within the tent during a long outing. Remember, moisture that is in your bag or clothing once you leave the bag will collect in the form of ice, or it may dissipate if not substantial. The goal in this instance is to keep moisture within your sleeping bag and clothing to a minimum and that is what makes owning a sleeping bag that allows moisture to pass through readily so important.

Rule number five is: adjust the heat within your body and extremities before you retire to the sleeping bag.

A sleeping bag insulates – that's it. If you put something cold into a sleeping bag, then the bag will attempt to keep it cold until you introduce a heat source that will change the dynamic of temperature from cool to warm within the sleeping bag. Your goal is to go to the bag with warm extremities and an elevated core temperature, therefore allowing your sleeping bag a 'jump start' at keeping you warm by introducing it to a heat source – you.

Never, ever go to sleep cold if you can help it, or it will take forever, if it happens at all, for the bag to warm you. This is one of the most important aspects of sleeping warm in the cold. We usually stand or sit around discussing the events of the day until we feel a chill or are overcome by fatigue, and then we decide to go to sleep. This practice inhibits us from warming up within the sleeping bag in short time. Do not go to bed until the blood is flowing. That means run in place outside your tent if necessary. Going to bed warm means you've only got one more chore to attend to in order to remain warm for most of the night – a midnight snack!

Rule number six: consume high-calorie foods just before you attempt to fall asleep. Nuts, cured meat and cheese are a few of these, and are each high in fat calories. Fat calories burn slowly and will allow you to sustain the warm condition that you entered the bag with throughout most of the night. Failure to properly fuel your body is like beginning a three hundred mile trip in your car with only a quarter-tank of gas. The car runs fine while there is fuel to burn, but once the fuel runs out – it shuts down. Just as your inner furnace will shut down, causing you to sleep chilled when otherwise you would have been warm. Don't run out of gas in the middle of the night!

Speaking of 'middle of the night' – should you get the urge to perform a necessary bodily function at some time before your intended wake-up – then do so. Holding it will only cause your body to heat unnecessary waste, which is itself a waste of precious calories.

The last detail may be one of the most important.

Rule number seven: always, always wear a fleece or wool stocking cap while in your sleeping bag. Heat is lost rapidly from your head at all times, but especially during sleep. Additionally, learn the mechanics of cinching the opening of your bag to limit the loss of precious heat from around your head and shoulders. Heat lost can never and will never be recovered, so limit it at the zippers or closures. These are the natural weak points where heat integrity is concerned, however all good bag makers have draft tubes or closures built in to reduce the amount of heat lost.

Attention to each detail will grant the probability that you will sleep warm and to the capabilities of your sleeping bag. It is easy to blame the bag when you are chilly, but remember, sleeping bags don't perform miracles. If you place a warm, clean-burning, properly fueled body into a capable, properly sheltered and insulated bag, you will be well on your way to 'La La Land.' Just climb in and start counting sheep – Alaska Dall sheep, that is.

I am currently and will always be the Alaska product representative for Wiggy's Outdoor Products. Wiggy's is located in Grand Junction, Colorado, and has been making the finest sleeping bags in the industry since 1987.

A patented laminating process makes "Lamilite®" insulation, which is utilized in all of Wiggy's products, so special. When wet, it will maintain its insulating qualities – but it won't be wet for long.   Silicone coated, the insulation is hydrophobic, repelling moisture away from the wearer.   Moisture being a major factor on all Alaska hunts, it is very important to take only clothing and insulating gear that will out-perform the elements.

Wiggy's sleeping bags are washable, and are guaranteed for life against material breakdown.   You simply cannot own a finer sleeping bag, and thousands of Alaskans trust their lives to Wiggy's bags.

If you are interested in owning a Wiggy's bag, give me a call. I own the *Wiggy's-Alaska!* retail store in Anchorage, Alaska, but I do not limit my customers to the confines of a border.   With a phone call, I will gain another loyal Wiggy's customer, and you will gain a valuable friend in Alaska.   Hopefully, I've made it perfectly clear how important it is to have a friend in Alaska!

Visit www.Wiggys.com for ordering information or a catalog. Or contact me in Anchorage, at (907) 336-1330.

Innovative Gear for Hunters

Levels of gear effectiveness and utility affect the hunt by allowing the hunter to place more energy into the focus of the hunt, which is the taking of game. Time spent in the struggle to maintain a comfortable operating level, although a valuable aspect of the overall hunting experience, reduces the time spent in the hunt. Therefore, when using less than favorable gear, you are becoming more of a utilitarian by squeezing every ounce of efficiency from your gear, but less of a hunter. On the other hand, if said gear is the most efficient that money can buy, then the engaged party spends more time in the hunt and less time worrying about utility and restoring comfort.

By designing a gear list that maximizes efficiency, the hunter is increasing the probability of a successful hunt because the time spent hunting increases. Once becoming cold and wet, especially in Alaska, the desire to hunt at or near a level that will produce a positive result is compromised. The will to hunt will be broken, and all that will be important is returning to the state of comfort that allowed a focused hunting experience.

Advances in gear design and function-ability have come a long way since Alaska was pioneered wearing cotton and wool. What worked then can and will certainly work now, however the amount of hunting competition in the early years of Alaska was negligible compared to current levels. For that reason, hunters must now direct unbroken attention in a limited allotted time toward making a hunt successful, and with gear that operates at peak efficiency. Each moment in Alaska, as a visitor, will be precious. Maximize those moments by coming prepared.

Sleeping Bags

One overlooked aspect of a hard hunt is a good night's rest. Very often it may be necessary to sleep damp, in cool conditions, after a rigorous day of side-hilling, stream-crossing, climbing, and glassing for endless hours through mind-draining optics. A rejuvenation period for the body (sleep) will be a necessity to restore peak operating levels in a physical sense. Therefore come armed with a sleeping bag that will provide that sound sleep during the most varied of conditions.

A sleeping bag brought to Alaska should be of synthetic construction and insulation. Synthetic bags dry much quicker than down (feather) insulated bags once becoming wet. That will be important to you for a number of reasons:

A bag constructed with down insulation will contain any moisture it is exposed to, and when not directly exposed to moisture, like rain, it will trap the perspiration that your body expels through the pores of your skin during sleep. Over time, this buildup will cause the bag to perform poorly because its insulating qualities are being diminished by the moisture that it is becoming saturated with, and the bag will become heavier also. The inner furnace of the hunter will then be robbed of precious heat, causing more uncomfortable rest. If a down-insulated bag is accidentally introduced to a river or lake during travel, then it is immediately rendered useless until it is dried completely. That can have dangerous consequences at worst, and offer an uncomfortable situation at best. Figure two days of dry weather, consecutive, for complete drying of a down insulated bag to happen. Two beautiful days consecutive, my friends, cannot be ordered in Alaska, and can only be delivered on chance.

For that reason, it is important that the synthetic bag contain insulation that has been silicone treated, allowing the largest and tiniest of moisture molecules and vapors to pass readily through the bag. A bag of this construction is considered hydrophobic, which means that it does not like water.

Loft is another vital feature, in that a loftier bag will increase the distance between the sleeper and the cooler air surrounding the bag. Continuous, extruded-filament insulation maintains loft more effectively than chopped-staple insulation, even after long periods of compression or after extended use. The fibers of the insulation chosen should not separate or clump, which can cause cold spots or areas of decreased efficiency within the bag. Clumping and shifting is most efficiently eliminated by a laminating process that adheres the lining to the insulation, and not by the series of stitching that holds most bags' insulation in place. Where there's stitching, there's compressed insulation, and therefore a cold spot in the bag.

Further, the composition of the shell and lining are equally important, and should be comprised of materials with a proper thread-count to promote a water molecule's passing through the bag. The construction of the shell and lining of sleeping bags is often overlooked, which causes more moisture to be captured even when the insulation is performing adequately.

There is only one sleeping bag company, made famous for its laminated insulation and outstanding sleeping bags.

The name of the insulation that I have recommended is Lamilite®, and the brand of sleeping bag that should accompany the hunter to Alaska is a *Wiggy's* brand sleeping bag. In my opinion, time wasted contemplating purchase of any other brand of sleeping bag to bring to Alaska is time wasted - period.

This is not an advertisement – it's the real deal.

I believed in Wiggy's outdoor products long before I became the Alaska representative. Claims that I may gain personally from your bringing a Wiggy's bag to Alaska are true, however I myself would never leave my Alaska home with any other brand. Simply ask yourself if you trust Marc Taylor...

Technologically Advanced Game Bags

Let's say that you've managed a successful hunt, which includes a downed animal, and it is relatively early as far as the total time allotted for your trip. For instance, day two of a ten-day hunt. Congratulations are in order for sure; however you must now work diligently to protect the game meat from spoilage and infestation for a full eight or nine days before it can be properly refrigerated.

A tool that has been developed to assist the hunter in this monumental task is the synthetic game bag. One particular brand, the *Technologically Advanced Game Bag*, or *T.A.G. Bag*, is made by *Pristine Ventures* of Fairbanks, Alaska. These bags are made from a synthetic called Game-Vent, which allows lightweight, breathable protection for the meat.

Being of synthetic construction, and therefore being considered hydrophobic, these bags will dry more readily, allowing the meat to remain dry. Washable and re-usable!

Again, the thread count and composition of Game-Vent is what makes it special, and T.A.G bags will soon become the standard for Alaska game bags. Contact me, or Pristine Ventures directly at www.PristineVentures.com for more information.

Cool and dry game meat is a major goal once the animal is taken, and not only are you morally and ethically responsible for the protection and transportation of the meat to the table, but you are also required by Alaska law to properly transport all edible meat from the field.

Hunters are held accountable for the meat that returns from the hunt, as well as the meat that does not. It is advisable to utilize any product that will further your successful fulfillment of this requirement, and T.A.G. Bags are a great start.

Citric Acid

An additional aid in the recovery and transportation of game meat from the field is Citric Acid. Combining the Citric Acid with water makes a solution, which is then applied liberally to the exposed surface of the meat. The solution lowers the Ph (acidity level) of the surface of the meat, rendering it unattractive to flies which may lay eggs on or near the surface of the meat. The eggs hatch into larvae (maggots), which then consume rotting meat in the natural cycle of becoming flies themselves.

Infestation can ruin large amounts of meat, and all meat bags should be checked daily to limit infestation if not prevent it entirely.

Citric acid will soon be widely available, and is currently available directly from *Wiggy's-Alaska!* in Anchorage. Arrange for purchase of citric acid near your hunting destination for ease of travel, then once in the field – utilize it!

Transportation of Meat and Gear

It is relatively easy to quickly attach yourself to the mantra, "Hunting is life." And if we are fortunate, our hunts will continue well into the octogenarian stage of life. Measures must be taken, however, to assure that level of success can be a reality, and properly maintaining our bodies during the more productive years is one of the keys to that success.

Since moving to Alaska, I have noticed a disturbing trend that is detrimental to long-lasting hunting health – packing excessively heavy-weight loads.

I've seen small- and large-framed adults, in an effort to save overall steps, carry extremely heavy loads for distances that make even pack mules cringe. Entire sheep and goats are carried from mountains stuffed in their entirety in the bottom of, or on the outside of the same pack that carries the camp and food. I am no "sissy" when it comes to packing, but I can assure you that the care of my knees is not overlooked when contemplating how to get my sheep off the mountain or my moose back to the lake. The care of my knees will not be compromised.

My only questions are – Why the torture on your knees and back? And... Are you in that much of a hurry to retire from hunting?

Our knees contain ligaments, cartilage, tendon and bone, all operating in delicate physo-mechanical concert to assist us in moving our bodies and heavy loads forward. A metal mechanical joint would surely wear out under such stresses, however, our knees have ways of repairing slight wear and tear through healing – if properly taken care of, that is.

Heavy loads in excess of 120 pounds should always be split into at least two loads in order to properly prevent strain on the knees and lower back. I accomplish this by carrying into the field a complete freighter frame for the hauling of meat and trophy. This "extra frame" travels on the outside of my internal-frame pack during walk-ins, and because of the packs that I have chosen, I can still keep the total weight of my empty pack and extra frame to under 8 pounds!

If there are only two loads, camp and meat, the loads are carried out in relays. In this manner, I walk three times farther, but under less stress per step. I find that fewer extended rests are needed and the overall fatigue, during, and for up to six weeks after the hunt (tendonitis), are less.

Back to the knees – anytime I am in possession of an extremely heavy pack, I am wearing *Ace* brand knee braces. These are made of neoprene, and will save the life of your knees! The inner mechanics of the knees are held in their proper places and overall wear and tear are minimal with their use.

I plan to hunt well into my '70's, through proper care of my knees NOW.

Short – Magnums

There is a ballistic explosion of shorter, fatter cartridges that pack near long-action levels of performance. The impact on the hunting experience is not monumental, as long-magnums remain very popular among hunters in all areas of the country. Short-mag's are still worth a mention here for a couple of reasons:

Shorter cartridge length will mean that rifles will be equipped with shorter, lighter receivers. The overall weight savings will be perceived in the field, especially in the lighter, more compact mountain rifles.

Case capacity will be slightly less, however performance characteristics remain near the same as the longer-action cousins because shorter cases means more efficient powder ignition once ignited. Quicker ignition, whether utilizing slow- or quick-burning powder, is more efficient, often producing a more consistent result. A sloppy shooter will still be a sloppy shooter, but a good shot may become more accurate.

I am personally a fan of shorter bolt manipulation. Here's why: The bolt of long-action rifles often travels too far to the rear during extraction and chambering, causing an interruption in stock weld between shots for the shooter. This is especially perceivable when utilizing scopes with shorter eye relief, when a cheek pad is present, or when length-of-pull has been shortened on a long-action rifle. Proper bolt manipulation is crucial for follow-up shots, and stock weld should not be interrupted while acquisition of the target is still important.

Magazine capacity will be diminished by one, due to the fatter case diameter of short-magnum cartridges. Therefore the shooter must get the job done with one less shot. I can handle that.

Short-magnums are a pleasure to shoot overall, and they have earned a permanent place in my very exclusive hunting arsenal.

Expedition Rivercraft

Chances are that you'll be contemplating the use of an inflatable canoe or raft to access the more remote rivers of Alaska during your hunt. Even during a hunt on or near the shore of a lake, an inflatable can be a valuable asset, allowing you to access the far shore with less *footprint*, or move the meat of a downed animal closer to camp with minimal effort.

S.O.A.R. Inflatables, in partnership with Larry Bartlett of Pristine Ventures, have created the S.O.A.R. *Pro-Pioneer*, an inflatable canoe capable of transporting 1,500 pounds of payload in a craft with a weight of only 80 pounds! That is important to the hunter because now we are able to meet fly-in hunt weight requirements with an inflatable craft onboard – drastically increasing our success rate as hunters.

The Pro-Pioneer has an overall length, when inflated, of 16 feet. The inflated diameter of its two main tubes is 14 inches, and it is 46 inches wide at the center. The Pro-Pioneer is built for two paddlers, but can be easily steered by one due to its sleek design.

These craft can be rented on a daily-basis at your intermediate hunting destination, or can be purchased directly by contacting Pristine Ventures at www.PristineVentures.com. Contact me for more information about renting a Pro-Pioneer in the Anchorage area.

Oar Saddle

Larry Bartlett has teamed up with *Rocking R Designs* to eliminate the bulky, heavy and sloppy-performing rowing frame. The end result is the *Oar Saddle®*.

It can best be described as a compact, lightweight, portable and durable rowing platform for inflatable boats. The transfer of energy is incredible, giving the boater the utmost in propulsion and control.

This apparatus is state-of-the-art, constructed of heavy grade aluminum that straddles the raft tube, lashing down with cam-buckle webbing and D-rings that come with the kit. All aspects of the Oar Saddle are adjustable to allow maximum power transfer due to the custom fit and proper oar lock height adjustability.

In utilizing the Oar Saddle, the boater/hunter has just considerably lightened the overall load, and added performance and maneuverability unmatched in conventional rowing frame design.

Contact *Rocking R Designs* at *www.OarSaddle.com* for more information, or when renting a craft for your float hunt, ensure that it comes equipped with the patented Oar Saddle.

My Pro Pioneer and I never leave home without it.

Titanium Goat

This is beginning to look more like a catalog than a book, however my commitment is to provide the most up-to-date information on gear and equipment to accompany you on your Alaska hunt.

A recent addition to the demanding Alaska hunter's gear list in the Titanium Goat Vertex 6.

This is a single-walled, floorless, one-pole tent, conical in design for maximum space utilization and wind resistance. The main body is constructed of silicone impregnated nylon for waterproof integrity. At six-feet tall, it provides seventy-nine square feet of floor space, which is roomy enough for two hunters and nearly all of their gear.

This tent weighs only three pounds!

I lived in this tent for one week on my most recent sheep hunt, and I was very impressed with the roominess and pack-ability. The weight of the tent, when split between two hunters, is practically *negligible* for pack-in hunting.

Contact *www.TitaniumGoat.com* for more information.

We have listed in this chapter only a few of the innovations that have come about in order to assist in the gathering of memories.

The gear utilized by hunters will continue to evolve, making us more efficient at our deadly endeavors. Only hunting with respect, reverence, and within established regulations will our place as hunters be assured forever.

Photo courtesy of Dan Frost

Titanium Goat Vertex 6

Photo courtesy of Bill Dean

Pro-Pioneer by S.O.A.R

When Things Go Terribly Wrong

Despite heroic efforts to prevent tragedy or disaster associated with an Alaska hunt, it can happen. It is better to be prepared mentally for that outcome, rather than never to have heard a story about a hunt gone wrong.

In the relatively short time that I have lived in Alaska, I have been fortunate enough to meet the best of people. Alaskans new and old are very sharing of their experiences, and there is no shortage here of tales of bad dealings with weather, equipment, bears, water, and just about every aspect of a hunt. I listen with a tuned ear to catch each detail in order that I may be better prepared to deal with tragedy when it strikes. This chapter will contain some of those word-of-mouth learnings.

Transporter Problems

Most transporters work hard to fulfill their obligations to safely carry you and your gear to the field. That is their business and they cannot continue to do business in this word-of-mouth world if you are not talking good about them and their services. However, sometimes there are circumstances beyond their control. A short list of possibilities would include weather, equipment failure, and yes, even terrorist attacks.

I once sat patiently for two days waiting to get into the bush because all air traffic had been shut down. You remember that, it was 9/11/01. That was two complete days of my hunt gone – never to be recovered. There were hunters waiting to get to the animals as well as hunters with animals waiting to get back to town; all were anxious that events were not unfolding exactly as planned.

Be extremely patient and courteous when hold-ups impede your progress. Flight services operate on tight timetables and often get backed up due to inclement weather. Your ranting and raving about your hunt schedule will fall on deaf ears, and you will no longer be a welcome customer.

Confirm everything before boarding an aircraft to be taken to the hunt area. Fly-overs, pick-up date, and movement of meat are just a few of the main points. If it concerns you, or has potential to mess up your hunt plan – talk about it. That includes having a weather contingency. If a front is moving in that will last for three days, would you want the transporter to pick you up early or late? Have a definite plan that is understood by all.

One means of removing all doubt is by staying in communication with the transporter while in the field. A great way to accomplish that is by satellite telephone. From the hunt site, meat pick-ups can be arranged, injuries or emergencies that occur during the hunt can be reported, and weather can be planned for.

It's a great feeling knowing exactly when pick-up will happen. It's an even better feeling to share your new bull moose with your buddy who backed out of the hunt at the last minute. He can listen in real time as you stretch the tape measure beyond sixty inches across the palms of your bull. The hunt pays for itself in a moment like that. I've done it.

Arrange for the rental of a satellite phone and share the expense among all the members of the hunting party.

Equipment Failure

The hunting party is responsible for the serviceability and utility of all gear associated with the hunt. This includes rented gear in the case of drop hunts. It is no one's fault but your own if you arrive at the hunt site with incomplete gear. I'm certain that the outfitter of the hunt would not intentionally omit the tent poles from your shelter kit, but it has happened. Do not expect a refund of any monies if you fail to check your field gear.

Ensure that the stove works before going to the field, and take an inventory of all the parts necessary to erect your shelter. Check the rented raft for holes, seam openings, and a complete repair kit. Patches will do you no good on the river without the glue necessary to secure the patch to the craft.

A hunting buddy and I once hiked thirteen miles into the mountains in search of sheep. I carried everything for ten days of hunting and comfort on my back. My buddy carried everything as well – except a spoon to eat the freeze-dried meals with. Miserable.

The small things can have a great effect on your overall experience, so check and re-check your gear list against what is actually in your pack.

Weather

Do a thorough investigation of what to expect in the hunting area at the time of the hunt. Then subtract twenty degrees and add five days of rain and fog. Now you're ready.

Problematic Bears

Unless you are on a bear hunt, it is not advisable to shoot a problematic bear unless you are in certain fear for your life. Bears are hunted pretty aggressively in Alaska, and therefore have an innate fear of humans. However, there is always that rogue bear that will ruin your hunt if he is allowed to.

If you have killed a bear in self-defense, then you must skin the bear, remove the skull, and report directly to the Alaska Department of Fish and Game to surrender the bear and file a full report of the events that led to your shooting the bear. You may be fined if it is found that you could have prevented killing the bear, so only do so if in danger of being attacked.

Bear attacks are relatively rare in Alaska, so you will be looked upon as a suspect until you have proven self-defense. Fear of a bear is not a reason to kill a bear. Fear of being attacked may be a reason if the bear is about to or has made contact with you.

If you allow a bear to be comfortable with your presence, he is well on the way to eventually tearing up your camp. Make every effort to scare a bear out of your valley when you first are made aware of its presence.

Storing your meat far from camp and out of sight will temp a marauding bear to investigate and eventually claim your meat. I personally store my meat close to camp, and at a distance that it can be defended from raiding. That distance is negotiable, but I usually ensure that it is far enough away that I can defend myself in the event of a charge.

Make every effort not to startle a bear in close quarters. A startled bear will turn and fight, so your best defense is to keep this situation from happening. If the thought has entered your mind that, "A bear could come crashing through here at any time", then chances are the current situation is not an ideal one. Influence the event that is about to happen by announcing your presence, whenever possible.

Always keep a firearm within reach once an animal is down, and particularly when meat is stored near camp.

Never leave meat in a raft overnight, or transportation plans will be altered once a bear tears up the raft to get to the meat.

I've included this section because bear encounters are a realistic probability. More often than not, a bear will be spotted at some time during a hunt, especially in open country or on rivers. Remember, fear and danger are two distinctly different mind sets. Treat bears with utmost respect at all times, and you may be allowed to pass unmolested.

Cold Water

The exploding popularity of rafting Alaska's wild rivers for the purpose of hunting has increased the amount of traffic that the waterways receive. More hunters mean more drownings. Therefore, it is of extreme importance that the rivers of Alaska be taken with deadly seriousness. Alaska rivers run fast, deep, and cold.

An overturned raft or being swept away during a crossing means that you have just gone from a hunting experience to a survival experience. Only once hunters and hunting gear are dry and warm will the hunt continue.

Always have a fire-producing element on your person, not stuffed away in your pack. It should be water-proof and reliable.

Make a contingency plan in case you and your partner are separated. Will you meet at the point of separation, or downstream? This should be understood before launching your raft or crossing a stream or river.

Adherence to Regulations

The hunt becomes tainted as soon as you decide to hunt outside the established regulations. Whether you actually get away with the infraction or not makes no difference – the hunt is forever tainted.

We all have lapses of judgment, but banish the thought while it is still a thought and before it becomes an action. In the grand order of things, the outcome will be more pleasant without being successful than to count yourself successful yet stand a broken man against the rules of fair sportsmanship.

Your safe arrival in Alaska is only the first leg of your journey. Count each successful event as a victory, and take note of improvements that can be made on future trips. One of the glories of being human is the ability to learn from experience, so capitalize on that gift.

Moose Hunting Tactics - 301

One of the more electrifying moments to be experienced in Alaska is one created solely of your own achievement. Few moments can equal those spent in the close company of the largest of the deer species – *Alces alces gigas,* or gigantic Alaska moose; a bull moose that *you* have called to within range!

In *Book One* I recommended the *"Love, Thunder and Bull"* series of moose calling videos by Wayne Kubat as the leading reference for your preparations for any upcoming moose hunt, whether it be in Alaska or Maine.   I still stand by that urging, but with renewed vigor.

In the last two years I have formed an acquaintance of Wayne Kubat, and I can name no other hunter of Alaska with more knowledge, respect, reverence and drive than the founder of *Alaska Remote Guide Service.*   Wayne is an often and welcome guest at *Wiggy's-Alaska!,* and he even has his own coffee cup hanging near the coffee pot! Discussion during his visits always turns to moose hunting strategy, and the air fills with moose theory, biology, physiology and vocalizations.

This man is passionate about his moose hunting, and at first handshake I was gripped by his expertise in the field of calling moose. Allow me to share some of **my** deepest secrets:

Get His Attention and Hold It!

Moose are certainly not the brightest creatures on the planet, but they aren't the dimmest, either. One of my first observations about moose, however, is that they have a rather short attention span.

I've repeatedly stated that I believe a moose can be "pulled," given the right circumstances, for a distance of five miles or more by skilled calling. Those circumstances will include:

- *Ability of the call to be projected to the distant moose* – For this you'll need a "Moose Magnet", which resonates the call at an elevated pitch, allowing the sound to reach him and get his attention.

- *Willingness to respond* – This will depend on the stage of the rutting activity that moose are in.

- *The caller's ability to hold his attention and make him come to the imitated calls* – The caller's aggressiveness, patience and willingness to believe that the calling is working and the realization that only time and distance stand between the hunter and his shooting opportunity.

If you've ever seen a moose turn his head toward your calls, he is marking your position, and can come exactly to the spot you are standing on without the aid of a GPS. Utilizing his antlers to assist his ears, the moose will gather the sound and estimate the distance to its maker. At that time, the intensity of response will be dictated by his energy level and his perception of your presence as a threat or potential mate. Become increasingly more enticing to him and don't allow his attention to stray from you.

Calling is certainly not a continual thing, and sessions are timed throughout the day. Time of day, temperature, cloud cover, precipitation and wind activity will dictate your level of calling.

Once the moose is rested, he will continue to feed. It is the caller's responsibility to remind him to feed in *THIS* direction, and not wander away.

Assume that your calls have been heard and work hard to maintain the moose's desire to get to your hunting area as a destination. Once his attention has been gained, you'll have to maintain it. Other moose encountered in his movement toward your position will become barriers to his arrival, so it is important to be *enticing*.

Sound Like Moose

Ever hear a moose cough? They do it. How about sneeze? Yep, they do that too, but they don't talk about wives or football games, so talking must never be heard by the moose that you are hunting. Once the plane leaves the lake, you should be whispering from then until the last tag is filled. But only if you're serious about getting your moose.

When moose hunting, unlike whitetail hunting, it is not important to be deathly afraid of making a sound, but it is important to know what sounds attract moose and what sounds will drive them away. Your cough will not drive them away as long as it is in concert with other natural moose sounds being made in your "area of influence".

In moving to your calling/hunting area from camp, don't tip-toe there, rather sound like *moose walking there*. I have a certain traveling call that I use, and it sounds like, *"Wwuahk."* Repeat it every ten steps or so, very softly, and go out of your way to break a branch here and there or maybe brush an imitated antler lightly against a tree. Breaking branches is a GREAT thing, and is an excellent way for the hunters to break up what will seem to be an uneventful day.

Moose have been known to "sneak" up to a hunter when he least expects it, but more often they make the noises that we would if we were "ditty-bopping" through the woods. Without the whistling, of course! If a twelve hundred pound moose can sneak up to within bow range of you on a moose hunt, then some serious reevaluation is necessary on your part. Don't let it happen!

One of my favorite tactics is to strip leaves from the end of tender branches, imitating the sound of *a moose stripping leaves from tender branches.* Imagine that. Do this from thick cover within your calling area so that your ruse cannot be spotted readily. It's very effective, and if nothing else you'll assure yourself that the stripping of those leaves was the deciding factor in that bull coming in.

The idea is to put distant moose at ease by convincing them that you are a *group* of moose lounging in the area. His approach will not be totally lackadaisical as a result, but he will be expecting to contact other moose near where you are and his first indication that something is wrong will be when, *BAAAM*, your Nosler Partition slams into his chest!

Moose are very gregarious. They like company. During the rut they like to fight and/or "engage in breeding activity", so if you listen closely, your first indication that your bull is on the way will be just what I've asked you to sound like – a breaking branch, or a soft *"Wwuahk"*. When you first hear that sound, engage him with whatever call brought him to you – bull or cow. When he knows that you are close, he'll begin to tear up the trees separating you and him in an effort to show his dominance. *This* is when your heart will really begin to beat, and if he's legal, your shooting opportunity will be near. Don't blow it.

Not Blowing It

Once the bull is in close, but not close enough for the shot, it will be up to the caller to **gauge his desires**. He will be looking for a fight, or he will be looking for some quick lovin', but usually not both, so you'll need to determine which activity he's more receptive to.

If the bull is in sight, but out of range, give him a bull "grunt". If he thrashes bushes and continues, well there you are... he's a fighter!

In the event he turns and runs a few paces but then stops to look back; he's been whipped recently, and is probably sneaking in to steal the cow that you convinced him that you are, so try a soft "cooing" sound of a cow.

If the shooter is a bowhunter, this will be a critical time, and the hunter will need to be between the caller and the moose in order to pull the moose into the vicinity of the hunter *unguarded*. The bull's senses will be on sharp alert, and his approach *unaware* that you are human will be critical.

No metallic sounds!

Separate the Calling Areas

Do not make the imitated sounds of a cow and a bull from the exact same location. Within your calling/hunting area, establish what will be "bull ground" and what will be "cow ground." The distance between these two specific areas should be at least fifty yards and not more than seventy-five yards. Your vantage/viewing point should be within eyesight of both areas in order to cover them both effectively with your rifle or bow.

Separating these two areas, which a listening bull can pinpoint with incredible accuracy, will allow him to choose which area to approach based upon his temperament and stage of rut. If he wants to beat off a challenger, he will come promptly to your established *bull area*. Most likely he'll be attempting to steal a cow, so watch the *cow calling area* closely and plan a shot should he step into or near it. Things will happen really fast once he decides, so be ready to act when the ground starts shaking and the alders start crashing!

I'm not joking. If you get a big rush from calling in a wild turkey, imagine what it is going to feel like with a twelve-hundred pound bull moose bellowing steam just yards away...

Most Productive Hunting Time

The key word is *productive.*

Forcing yourself to hunt from before dawn to after dusk is exhausting. Effective, but exhausting, and attempting to do so on a moose hunt will only invite fatigue, angst and boredom. I'd like to introduce an alternative, but first I will explain my reasoning.

Moose are *ruminants*, which mean that they digest their

sustenance in steps. Extraction of nutrients from raw leaves, grass, twigs, etc. means that semi-digested "cud" must be regurgitated then re-chewed in a process called *ruminating.* It is also important to note that moose are active day *and* night, and especially active during the pre-rutting and rutting period. Therefore the most effective time to hunt moose is during the pre-rut and rut, and more specifically, during periods when they are not engaged in ruminating "cud chewing" activity.

The chewing of "cud" is not a chosen activity, it is a necessary activity. The members of the deer species must enter into a "down time" after eating or the food taken on will not be properly digested. One heck of a belly-ache.

It is widely believed that the most active time for moose to feed during the fall (hunting season) is during the cool nights. Generally, they will bed down *before* dawn and begin ruminating. That puts them back into an active phase just as the hunter is wearing out from looking through glasses for most of the morning with no result!

Begin your active hunting of moose at around ten o'clock in the morning and continue uninterrupted until after dark. This will allow you to "come to work" rested, with a full belly from a proper camp breakfast. It works totally against what we've come to expect of hunting, which is intensifying our efforts to coincide with dawn and dusk active times, however, among serious moose hunters, the middle of the day, especially on cloudy, cool and windless days, is the most productive.

The calling session conducted just before coming back to camp on the night before put the bull into an overnight feeding in the direction of your calling. Theoretically, he has "camped out" just outside your area of influence. The break from morning calling activity that you take will drive him crazy with curiosity, and prevent "overexposure" of your calls. Your return to the calling/hunting area at mid-morning will coincide with his mid-day stretch and investigation of the "group of moose" that we have convinced him are in this area. *BAAAAM!* End of story. Let the tagging, quartering and hauling begin, and we'll be done before the wolves and bears get the first whiff of the gutpile.

Of course, it is pretty smart to be on attentive lookout for the incoming bull moose at *all* times, even during the early hours, but a concentrated effort from mid-day on will allow a more focused exertion with less fatigue and boredom that an all-day hunt can incur.

The general moose hunting season closes in most of Alaska by the end of September, which is before the full-on-don't-sleep-don't-eat rut, so the "noon rush" strategy is sound and very effective.

Moose Hunting Tactics – 301

- Learn to "speak moose" with Wayne Kubat's videos
- Gain attention with aggressive calling
- Hold his attention and split your calling area
- Sound like a group of moose to make the approaching bull comfortable
- Be confident that your calling is working on the yet unseen, unheard bull moose
- Once contact is made, gauge his desires
- Entice him with those desires

- Take great pictures of him before and after the shot in order that he may be respected for generations!

Moose hunting is not an exact science, nor is it a science at all. There are many factors out of your control even when in the known presence of moose in your *area of interest.* If discipline is maintained within the hunters' camp and within the hunting area, your chance of moose unknown to you coming into shooting range will be greater – given that the moose are present and your imitated calls are effective.

Factors Out of Our Control

Weather – Moose do not go indoors during inclement weather. However, the effectiveness of even the greatest calling efforts will be diminished by rain and wind. Your focus must not be broken by less-than-ideal conditions, so remain persistent, convincing yourself that your imitated calls are working even if no response is evident.

Other moose – We cannot control the other moose that may wander into and out of our hunting area from time to time. If the bull that you are calling comes across a receptive cow, you will certainly be put on the back burner even with a perfect calling scenario. What you can do, however, is utilize the company of the other moose as an attractant, capitalizing on their presence by utilizing their ability to put the targeted moose at ease.

Other hunters – Yes, even in Alaska. Just when you believe that there must be no other hunter for a hundred miles, you'll spot that light across the lake at dark. The light of another hunting camp. Don't expect to be alone in Colorado during elk season, nor should you expect to be alone in Alaska during moose season. One can hope for that, but it cannot be assured.

The presence of other hunters should not be allowed to hinder your efforts to produce moose for the freezer and the taxidermist back home. It's not that there will be enough for everybody, as may be correct when hunting amongst hundreds of caribou, but *YOU* are the better hunter here. Now it is necessary to prove it.

The tips on moose strategy contained in this chapter are based upon my personal experiences in the presence of moose. I am neither a biologist nor a professional hunter, but I do consider myself a very successful moose hunter, armed with a thorough understanding of moose habitat, moose habits and my relationship to both when in pursuit of moose.

My thanks are extended to Wayne Kubat for "sparking the tinder."

For more information on the "Love, Thunder and Bull" series of moose calling videos, contact Wayne or Marilyn Kubat at:

Alaska Remote Guide Service

P.O. Box 874867

Wasilla, AK 99687

www.alaskaremote.com

Part III

The Final Breath

The Answer to the Question –
"Why Do I Hunt?"

I hunt because I am a very complex and evolved being, in touch with death, life, and the effect that each have on the other.

I hunt to enrich my life. To experience the kinships, the hardships and the challenges that hunting game animals provides.

I hunt to test myself, my limitations and my capabilities as a measurement of my endurance and skill in the environment of the hunted.

I hunt to feel the highs of exhilaration that I get when my hunts are successful.

I hunt to feel the depths of sorrow that I feel when my hunts are successful.

I hunt to participate in something greater than life. My participation in the death of an animal that I have hunted makes that animal, mentally and physically, forever a part of my being.

I hunt armed with more reverence and respect than bullets or broad heads.

I hunt because I am born, instinctively a predator, choosing to gather the meat that I need to sustain my life and the lives of my loved ones.

I hunt to feel alive.

I hunt because I am a hunter.

-- A simple question may lead to a very complex answer. Now, why do *you* hunt?

Photo courtesy of Dan Frost

Into goat country

Into sheep country

Life's great on top

Then there's the packing

Moose calling works!

Photo courtesy of Andy Sorensen at ajstudio@alaska.com

Photo courtesy of Jason Harding

See...

Photo courtesy of Roy Smith

Sometimes it's hard to Hunt Hard

Photo courtesy of David Keith

Photo courtesy of Matt Cooper

Come loaded for bear...

Photo courtesy of Heike Frost

No, REALLY loaded for bear!

The dirty work

Photo courtesy of David Keith

Photo courtesy of Adam Millburn

Magnificent caribou

Photo courtesy of Jason Harding

Photo courtesy of Dan Niedert

Sweet success

Photo courtesy of Jason Harding

Photo courtesy of Larry Bartlett

S.O.A.R. Pro – Pioneer

Photo courtesy of Kent Rotchy

Photo courtesy of Al Henderson

It gets no better than this

Photo courtesy of Tommy Camp

Photo courtesy of Andrew Lewis

Gotta do what you've gotta do...

Photo courtesy of Jason Eitutis

Photo courtesy of Stephen Bethune

Never give up

Photo courtesy of Dan Frost

A Sense of Belonging

From the first moment of your first hunt you probably felt "different". Not something that a person can put a finger on, but certainly a different feeling from then on.

If this hunt took place in the company of adults, then the feeling was even stronger. Whereas we may not possess the body weight or maturity in our youth to participate in the grown-up games such as the card game that your Mom or Dad held or the full-contact football that the older kids participated in, with hunting, you were allowed the same level of participation as the adults; and it made you feel good. It made you feel really good.

In the society in which we live it is common practice to faction-alize ourselves into groups. In youth, this may be by age, grade level, neighborhood or interest, but we form groups, each with a pride and sense of belonging unique to that group. The sense is an important part of emotional development and is a very important part of relationship building and bonding that follows us far into maturity.

The first time you were invited on the hunt, you may have been nervous or felt anxiety at being included in such a deadly game on an adult level. It may have been very important to show that you are worthy of the companionship of adults, where in this instance success is measured by an ability to cause death.

I find it very fascinating that we are introduced to deadly sport at a less-than-mature age. Often, the young human mind is not capable of processing the finality of death, as we feel so immortal in youth. Yet, when included, we deal death with a fervor far surpassing that of our adult mentors.

It can be argued, and it is my opinion, that there are levels of progression necessary during the introduction of a human to the dealing of death. If a hunter is encouraged at a young age to experience hunting as a progression, then the act of taking life will have a lesser effect on the overall being.

Your nine-year-old kid taking the life of a sparrow is not an earth-shattering event. Would we feel the same if that child lined up the sights of a high-caliber rifle on another human being?

Killing is an act. Hunting is an act. So what's the difference?

When we introduce a child to hunting we are allowing a participation far above the well-meaning intention of just getting the child out of the house or away from the television. We are introducing that child to death and to the causing of it, and that is a tremendous responsibility. The way that the mentoring adult nurtures the feelings that will follow will forever change a critical aspect of that child's development. The child may be disgusted at the act, or the child will experience a sense of pride or accomplishment. Both are healthy reactions and are glimpses into the psyche of the adult that the child will mature into.

The level of participation is dictated by the adult mentor.

A child will not ask to go on a Marco Polo sheep hunt. However, there are cases of children as young as ten years old being allowed to participate in such a hunt. Is that right or is that wrong?

The development of the healthy human mind is much faster than the development of the healthy human body. There are twelve-year-old children graduating from college, possessing the mental capacity and intellectual intelligence of fully mature adults. But in the hunting world, there are no twelve-year-old children capable of planning and executing a solo moose hunt. So why are we allowing children to merely pull the trigger on animals above their capacity to hunt in the true sense of the word? I think we agree that hunting is more than pulling a trigger, right? Yet we are convincing ourselves that our "little hunting buddy" is participating although there is a tremendous handicap being extended and a limited level of participation being required. We let them do the killing part.

You may feel good now about that young child of yours dropping that sheep, but where will it end? Will the child become bored after such accelerated accomplishment? My bet is that you won't have that hunting buddy on that level for very long.

Children pressed into growing up too rapidly have a tendency to "grow down" very rapidly as well. Be prepared for that. There is a "pageant mentality" present and growing among the brotherhood of hunters. We are smearing makeup on the faces of young children creating beauty many years beyond maturity, and we are smearing camouflage on the faces of young children creating killers many years below maturity.

You've heard this before – "Hunting as a progression".

I propose that we involve children on the level of mental

participation only to the extent that they are physically capable of participating under the same circumstances.

When your child can pack seven days of gear into the mountains, including an instrument of death, then your child is ready for that sheep hunt – but not until then. Otherwise, it is the child who is being utilized as the instrument of death by the adult, pressing achievement for a misdirected or selfish purpose.

I find that very few children are using the words "Sir" and Ma'am" in the company of adults, yet we expect them to have respect for their ability to cause death. Respect is taught, or *should* be taught at an early age. When your child has reached a level of respect, which allows him or her to address me as "Mr. Marc" without fail, then you may have yourself the makings of a young hunter in my eyes, given the correct avenue of progression. But until then it is best to instruct your child on proper behavior in the company of living adults rather than teaching them power in the company of dead animals.

This particular child's sense of belonging may be among other children, learning how to be a child first before being included as an equal among the adults.

It sounds as though I am uncomfortable with children in the sport of hunting. Entirely not true. I am eager to introduce your child and mine to the wonderful world of hunting Alaska, but only after basic lessons in the art and practice of dealing death have been understood and their sense of belonging in the company of adult hunters has been established.

As a matter of fact, this is not about children at all. I have met recently, young adults just entering into the hunting world who have less respect for life and death than the most basic of child hunters. "I just can't wait to kill something" is what I've heard. My answer to that is "We are at war, how about you go to Iraq and kill something." Of course this person is less prepared to enter into combat than to point a rifle at a caribou, and having no experience in the act of killing on a basic level, would likely be devastated by the killing of another human being. That is, if his life were not taken first.

The reason for this soldier being unprepared to cause death upon another human being is a lack of exposure to death. An exposure to hunting would have been a huge benefit to this soldier, beginning with the most basic of game animals and progressing to more complex, physically demanding hunts for thinking, man-fearing game.

Hunters are exposed to death, the causes of it and the effect that the death of an animal at the hunter's hands has on the hunter's being.

Our children need to be introduced to hunting at their own pace, with game animals appropriate to the skill levels of their minds, not their mechanics. A child can be taught to shoot well, but shooting is not killing and killing is not hunting. Don't we all preach that to the non-believers at every questioning?

It's as simple as an explanation. "Little Johnny, you can't drive, swear or get a job yet because you're not mature enough to belong in the adult world yet. Now, go gather your hunting stuff, we're going to Alaska so you can shoot a brown bear."

What's wrong with that picture?

But this is about *sense of belonging,* isn't it? We want to be included in something larger than the *self*. When you and your buddies hung out at the tree house as kids there was a special bonding that could not be duplicated. You were a part of something bigger, and the common glue was the experiences that you shared.

We still are a part of something bigger than *self*. A sense of belonging is one of the most basic human needs. Where a person finds that comfort varies, but hunters usually find solace only among other hunters; others who have caused death and can relate to that troubling notion.

It's a very good chance that if you are reading this, nearly your entire inner-most circle of friends is made up of hunters. We have an uncanny way of finding each other and are instantly bonded, regardless of the level of participation or experience.

One of the more important aspects of retaining that close sense of belonging is by participation. The dinners and fundraisers held by the various foundations and federation chapters are a great way to extend the circle of friends. With each event I attend, I leave with a renewed sense of having contributed beyond my meager accomplishments of the hunt. I meet new friends and acquaintances and make terrific hunting contacts from those whom I would never have met otherwise.

As hunters, we need to extend the hand of understanding and companionship to other hunters by seeking those who share our deadly interests and include them in our inner circle.

You know the feeling of being the only hunter at the party.

Now imagine the feeling of being the last hunter at the party.

Together, we must never allow that to happen.

About the Author

Marc Taylor lives in Anchorage, Alaska, and is the owner of *Wiggy's-Alaska!*, a retail store catering to lovers of the Alaska outdoors. He is a freelance writer, and will soon begin work on the third book in the *Hunting Hard...In Alaska!* series.

Please visit ***www.HuntingHardInAlaska.com*** for upcoming title releases, information about planning your Alaska adventure, or recent photos of Marc's Alaska adventures.

About the Illustrator

Larry Golden began drawing at the age of three years, creating non-artistic murals on the living-room walls of his home. Since then, he has never been far from a pencil and sketch pad.

Larry has worn many hats in his nearly fifty years of age; Preacher, Rancher, Taxidermist and Painter, each approached with a strong appreciation for the beauty that God created for us to enjoy.

Nationally recognized for his life-like sculptures and award-winning taxidermy, Larry is self-taught, crediting God for any talent or ability that he may possess.

Larry lives with his lovely wife, Lydia, in Palmer, Alaska where he and his son Micah tend to the family business – *About Wildlife Art Taxidermy*.

I was fortunate to meet Larry Golden at the 2005 Alaska Sportsman's Show, and he and I have become great friends. For more information about Larry's wildlife art, western art, or taxidermy, contact him directly at 907-745-2180.

My sincere thanks, Larry for the beautiful job you did with the illustrations in this book. -- Marc

Appendix

Author-preferred airlines that service Alaska:

Alaska Airlines
www.alaskaairlines.com
1-800-252-7522

America West Airlines
www.americawest.com

Northwest Airlines
www.nwa.com
1-800-225-2525

American Airlines
www.AA.com
1-800-433-7300

United Airlines
www.united.com
1-800-864-8331

Continental Airlines
www.continental.com
1-800-525-0280

Air Cargo Services out of Alaska:

Alaska Air Cargo
www.alaskaairlines.com
1-800-255-2752

Continental Air Cargo
1-800-525-0280

Airlines to destinations within Alaska:

Era Aviation
www.eraaviation.com
1-800-866-8394

Pen Air
1-800-448-4226

Air Cargo carriers within Alaska:

Northern Air Cargo
www.northernaircargo.com
1-800-727-2141

Pen Air Cargo
1-907-243-3322

Era Aviation
www.eraaviation.com
1-907-243-3332

Hotels and Inns:
All six of these Hotels/Inns are within close proximity of the airport and Lake Hood, and offer airport shuttle service.

Millennium Hotel Anchorage
www.millenniumhotels.com
1-907-243-2300

Westcoast International Inn
1-907-243-2233

Holiday Inn Express
1-907-248-8848

Long House Alaskan Hotel
1-907-243-2133

Marriott Courtyard
1-800-321-2211 or
1-907-245-0322

Best Western Barratt Inn
www.barrattinn.com
1-907-243-3131

Author-preferred local flight services and air taxi services:

I am only listing air services that I personally have had contact with, and would recommend. This is **not** meant to be a comprehensive list of the air services available to the Alaska hunter.

Alaska Air Taxi
www.alaskaairtaxi.com
1-907-243-3944

Alaska West Air
www.alaskawestair.com
1-907-776-5147

Natron Air (Soldotna)
www.natronair.com
1-877-520-8440

Jim Air
www.flyjimair.com
1-907-243-5161

Regal Air
www.alaska.net/~regalair
1-907-243-8535

Trailridge Air
www.trailridgeair.com
1-907-248-0838

Willow Air
www.matnet.com/~wilair
1-907-495-6370

Renew Air Taxi(Dillingham)
www.renewairtaxi.com

Gear Sources and Retailers, National:

Wiggy's-Alaska! (Anchorage)
1-907-336-1330

Cabela's
www.cabelas.com

Sportsman's Warehouse
www.sportsmanswarehouse.com

R.E.I.
www.rei.com

Wiggy's, Inc.
www.wiggys.com

Gear Sources and Retailers, Anchorage:

Sportsman's Warehouse
8681 Old Seward Highway
Anchorage 907-644-1400

Mountain View Sports
3838 Old Seward Hwy.
Anchorage 907-563-8600

Wal-Mart (Mid-Town)
3101 A. Street
Anchorage 907-563-5900

Wal-Mart (South Anchorage)
8900 Old Seward Hwy.
Anchorage 907-344-5300

Alaska Department of Fish and Game

www.state.ak.us/adfg
P.O. Box 25526
Juneau, AK 99802-5526

333 Raspberry Road
Anchorage, AK 99518
1-907-267-2100

Shipping of Antlers from Anchorage to Your Home:

Knight's Taxidermy   **Hunter-Fisher Taxidermy**
7329 Arctic Blvd.   822 W. International Airport Rd.
Anchorage, AK 99518   Anchorage, AK 99518
907-345-5501   907-561-1466

Additional Required Reading

Any and all books by Larry Kaniut. Purchase them at **www.kaniut.com**
Alaska by James Michener
Bear Hunting In Alaska and
Sheep Hunting in Alaska (Second Edition) by Tony Russ
Sheep Stalking in Alaska by Tony Russ **www.tonyruss.com**
A Complete Guide to Float Hunting Alaska (Second Edition) **and**
Caribou Hunting by Larry Bartlett   **www.pristineventures.com**
Moose Hunting in Alaska by Rich Hackenberg
Hunt 'em High by Duncan Gilchrist
Quest for Dall Rams by Duncan Gilchrist
Alaska's Wolf Man by Jim Rearden
Meditations on Hunting by Jose Ortega Y Gasset
Bloodties by Ted Kerasote
A Sand County Almanac by Aldo Leopold
Beyond Fair Chase by Jim Posewitz

Great DVD's

700 Miles Alone by Pack and Raft by Buck Nelson **www.bucktrack.com**
Love, Thunder and Bull I and II by Wayne Kubat **www.args.com**
Complete Field Care of Alaska's Big Game Animals and
Float Hunting Alaska by Larry Bartlett at
www.pristineventures.com

E-Sources

www.PristineVentures.com
    Hit the <u>Chat Room</u> link.

www.OutdoorsDirectory.com
    Hit the <u>Forums </u>link.

Order Form

Give the gift of *Hunting Hard...In Alaska!*
Order online at www.HuntingHardInAlaska.com, or
mail the form below.

_____ Signed copies of Book One
"Prepare Yourself To Hunt 'The Last Frontier'"

_____ Signed copies of Book Two
"The Soul of the Hunt"

_____ X $19.95 = _____
Shipping, add $4.00

Total _____

Payment by check or money order
Make payable to **Hunting Hard – Alaska Adventures**
8931 Jupiter Drive
Anchorage, AK 99507

Visa, MasterCard accepted

Marc, call me at ph#_____
For my Visa / MasterCard information
Ship to: _____ name

_____address

_____City, State, Zip

Personalize my book(s) to the following:

_____

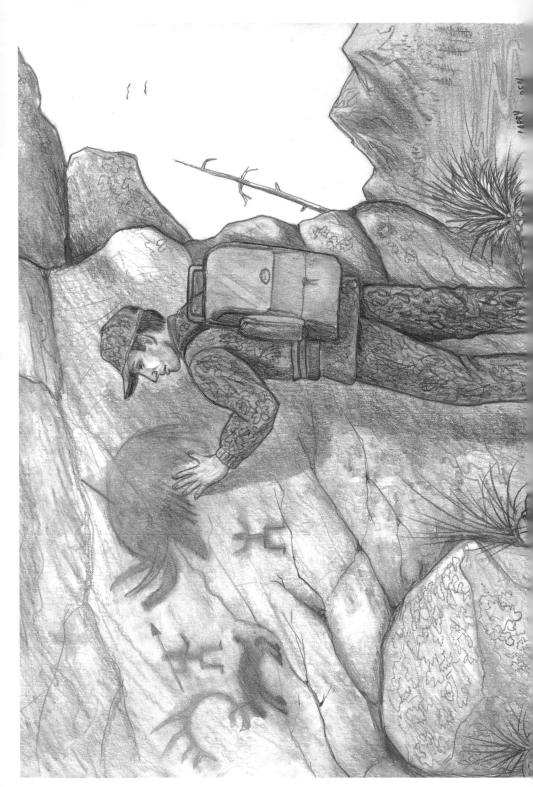

Go within.

Discover the depth
of your reverence
for the animals that you hunt.

Release the intensity
of your passion
for the hunt.

...And you will never
go without.

-- Marc